ROUND AND ROUND THE CROCHET HOOK

PATTERNS TO INSPIRE AND ADMIRE

EMILY LITTLEFAIR

Tuva Publishing
www.tuvapublishing.com

Address Merkez Mah. Cavusbasi Cad. No:71
Cekmekoy - Istanbul 34782 / Turkey
Tel: +9 0216 642 62 62

Round and Round The Crochet Hook

First Print 2017 / September

Content Crochet

Editor in Chief Ayhan DEMİRPEHLİVAN
Project Editor Kader DEMİRPEHLİVAN
Designer Emily LITTLEFAIR
Technical Editors Wendi CUSINS, Leyla ARAS, Büşra ESER
Graphic Designers Ömer ALP, Abdullah BAYRAKÇI, Zilal ÖNEL
Photograph Tuva Publishing, Emily LITTLEFAIR

ISBN: 978-605-9192-30-9

Printing House
Bilnet Matbaacılık ve Yayıncılık A.Ş.

TuvaYayincilik TuvaPublishing
TuvaYayincilik TuvaPublishing

CONTENTS

INTRODUCTION 7

PROJECT GALLERY 8

CROCHET BASICS AND TECHNIQUES 122

PROJECTS

WINNIE'S WONDERLAND BLANKET 12

GARDEN ROWS CUSHION 28

SUNNY CITRUS CUSHION 38

BLOOMING COASTERS 44

BLOOMING PLACEMAT 48

FLOWER PATCH CUSHION 52

DANCING AROUND IN CIRCLES 58

SWEET SUNSHINE DOILY 62

PRIMROSE PATCH RUG 68

STARS IN THE NIGHT SKY 74

DANDELION BOUQUET DOILY 80

FENCED AROUND WALL HANGING 86

LOOPING AROUND GARLAND 92

FLOWER PETALS CUSHION 96

LAZY DAISY SHOULDER BAG 100

STRING OF BLOSSOMS TABLE RUNNER 106

SPOTTY AND DOTTY GARLAND 112

PINEAPPLES AND LACE CUSHION 116

4

INTRODUCTION

In this book you will find designs that you can sit back and make in an afternoon. Quick and easy patterns that will add that personal touch to a room and make any house a home. Dress your table in coasters and placemats, colour coordinate your lounge room with different shaped cushions, or fill a blank wall with as many wall hangings as you like.

The designs use DMC Natura Just Cotton, which is a fingering weight yarn, or Natura XL a nice soft chunky yarn. However, you can change things up and make something in Natura XL that I designed in the fingering weight. Or you could turn most of the designs into wall hangings by adding them to rings or hoops.

Being a mum of three boys, I found it hard to find the time to crochet big projects so most of my designs take from a couple of hours to a couple of days to make.

I love that the possibilities are practically endless and the only limit is your imagination and how much yarn you currently have in your stash. Making something special from raw materials gave me such a great sense of accomplishment and happiness that I wanted to share it with other people.

I enjoy the entire journey of designing patterns, from discovering what's going to be in the next round, to designing smaller patterns made in the round that don't often become works-in-progress, but hot-off-the-hook finished pieces.

It's hard to imagine how a skein's worth of chain stitch when I was 11, has grown into a love of crochet so strong that it has resulted in this book.

I hope you enjoy crocheting these patterns as much I loved making them and that you too can have that sense of accomplishment and happiness that I feel when I complete a project.

Happy Hooking

Much Love,

Em xoxo

PROJECT GALLERY

P.12

P.86

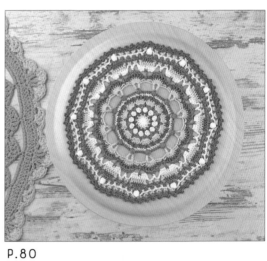

P.80

P.100

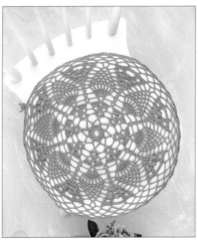

P.116

P.52

P.112

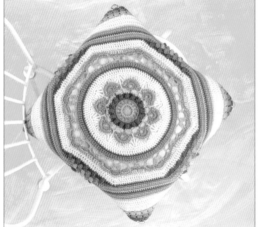

P.28

P.44

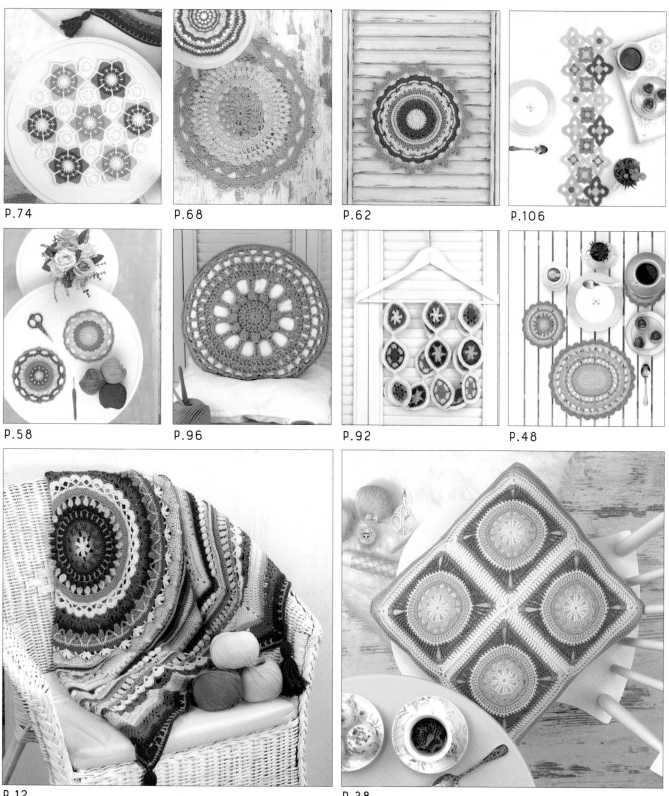

P.74

P.68

P.62

P.106

P.58

P.96

P.92

P.48

P.12

P.38

PROJECTS

WINNIE'S WONDERLAND BLANKET

Say hello to Winnie's Wonderland - my most treasured design in this book. I fell in love with this piece after about the fifth round. This love resulted in wanting to create something so beautiful, that everyone else would fall in love with it too. Everything about this blanket fills me with adoration… The colors I chose; the stitches I used; and most of all, how amazing it feels to hold and have in my hands. I named this design after a friend who helped me understand how to square up large circles. Now that I know how to do this, I will never forget it – nor will I forget my friend. I couldn't decide on a color palette, so I worked up two versions of the same pattern. To be honest, I cannot decide which one looks better. So, now I ask you… Will you make the blue or pink blanket?

Finished Size

38" (96.5 cm) square

FINISHED SIZE

38" (96.5 cm) square

MATERIALS

DMC Natura Just Cotton

Colors Used in Blue Blanket

Rose Layette (#06)	2 balls
Spring Rose (#07)	1 ball
Amaranto (#33)	1 ball
Blue Jeans (#26)	3 balls
Star Light (#27)	3 balls (plus 1 ball for Tassels)
Turquoise (#49)	1 ball
Acanthe (#81)	2 balls
Glacier (#87)	1 ball
Aguamarine (#25)	1 ball
Bleu Layette (#05)	1 ball
Lobelia (#82)	1 ball
Ble (#83)	1 ball

Colors Used in Pink Blanket

Rose Soraya (#32)	2 balls
Cerise (#62)	2 balls
Spring Rose (#07)	2 balls
Amaranto (#33)	2 balls
Rose Layette (#06)	1 ball
Malva (#31)	1 ball
Glacier (#87)	2 balls
Jade (#20)	2 balls
Ivory (#02)	1 ball
Salomé (#80)	1 ball
Gardenia (#36)	1 ball
Light Green (#12)	2 balls

Hook: Size E-4 (3.50 mm)

Scissors & Yarn Needle

PATTERN NOTES

1 A Magic Ring *(see Techniques)* can be used instead of the chain ring in Round 1.
2 All joins are slip stitches, unless otherwise indicated.3.
3 All new colors are joined with right side facing, unless otherwise indicated.
4 Weave in all ends as you go.
5 Standing stitches *(see Techniques)* can be used to start a round with a new color.
6 An invisible join *(see Techniques)* can be used at the end of a round to finish a color.
7 Lightly block finished blanket, if desired.

SPECIAL STITCHES

Join With Single Crochet (join with sc): With slip knot on hook, insert hook into stitch or space indicated and pull up a loop (2 loops on hook). Yarn over and pull through both loops on hook (first single crochet made).

Popcorn (pc): Work 5 dc in same stitch or space indicated, drop lp from hook, insert hook from front to back in first dc made, pull dropped lp through, ch 1 (to lock).

Front Post Treble Crochet: (FPtr): Yarn over hook twice, insert hook from front to back to front around post of indicated stitch, yarn over and draw up a loop, [yarn over and pull through 2 loops on hook] 3 times (tr made).

Beginning Four Treble Bobble (beg-tr4-bob): Ch 3, yarn over hook twice, insert hook in stitch or space indicated and draw up a loop (4 loops on hook), [yarn over, pull through 2 loops on hook] twice (2 loops on remain on hook), *yarn over hook twice, insert hook in same stitch or space and draw up a loop, [yarn over, pull through 2 loops on hook] twice; rep from * once more, yarn over, pull through all 4 loops on hook.

Four Treble Bobble (tr4-bob): Yarn over hook twice, insert hook in stitch or space indicated and draw up a loop (4 loops on hook), [yarn over, pull through 2 loops on hook] twice (2 loops on remain on hook), *yarn over hook twice, insert hook in same stitch or space and draw up a loop, [yarn over, pull through 2 loops on hook] twice; repeat from * twice more (5 loops remain on hook), yarn over, pull through all 5 loops on hook.

Three Treble Bobble (tr3bob): Yarn over hook twice, insert hook in stitch or space indicated and draw up a loop (4 loops on hook), [yarn over, pull through 2 loops on hook] twice (2 loops on remain on hook), *yarn over hook twice, insert hook in same stitch or space and draw up a loop, [yarn over, pull through 2 loops on hook] twice; rep from * once more, yarn over, pull through all 4 loops on hook.

Two Treble Bobble (tr2-bob): Yarn over hook twice, insert hook in stitch or space indicated and draw up a loop (4 loops on hook), [yarn over, pull through 2 loops on hook] twice (2 loops on remain on hook), yarn over hook twice, insert hook in same stitch or space and draw up a loop, [yarn over, pull through 2 loops on hook] twice (3 loops remain on hook), yarn over, pull through all 3 loops on hook.

Single Crochet Decrease: (sc2tog): Insert hook in first stitch or space indicated and draw up a loop (2 loops on hook). Insert hook in next stitch or space indicated and draw up a loop (3 loops on hook). Yarn over and pull through all 3 loops on hook.

Treble Decrease (tr3tog): Yarn over hook twice, insert hook in stitch or space indicated and draw up a loop (4 loops on hook), [yarn over, pull through 2 loops on hook] twice (2 loops on remain on hook), *yarn over hook twice, insert hook in next stitch or space and draw up a loop, [yarn over, pull through 2 loops on hook] twice; rep from * once more, yarn over, pull through all 4 loops on hook.

Back Post Double Crochet (BPdc): Yarn over hook, insert hook from back to front to back around post of indicated stitch, yarn over and draw up loop, [yarn over and pull through 2 loops] twice (double crochet made).

Double Treble (dtr): Yarn over hook three times, insert hook in stitch or space indicated and draw up a loop (five loops on hook). [Yarn over and pull yarn through two loops on hook] 4 times, until only one loop remains on hook.

Three-Chain Picot (p3): Chain 3, insert hook back into the center of the base stitch (through both the front loop and loop below the front loop), yarn over and pull through stitch and loops on hook (slip stitch made).

Back Post Treble Crochet (BPtr): Yarn over hook twice, insert hook from back to front to back around post of indicated stitch, yarn over and draw up loop, [yarn over and pull through 2 loops] three times (treble crochet made).

V-Stitch (one chains) (v1-st): Work (dc, ch 1, dc) in same stitch or space indicated.

V-Stitch (two chains) (v2-st): Work (dc, ch 2, dc) in same stitch or space indicated.

V-Stitch (three chains) (v3-st): Work (dc, ch 3, dc) in same stitch or space indicated.

Winnie's Wonderland Colours

Rnd	Blue	Pink	Rnd	Blue	Pink
1	Rose Layette	Glacier	34	Blue Layette	Salome
2	Spring Rose	Light Green	35	Amaranto	Gardenia
3	Amaranto	Jade	36	Spring Rose	Ivory
4	Amaranto	Jade	37	Lobelia	Cerise
5	Blue Jeans	Gardenia	38	Acanthe	Amaranto
6	Star Light	Spring Rose	39	Ble	Spring Rose
7	Star Light	Spring Rose	40	Ble	Spring Rose
8	Star Light	Spring Rose	41	Glacier	Rose Layette
9	Turquoise	Amaranto	42	Turquoise	Cerise
10	Star Light	Spring Rose	43	Star Light	Rose Soraya
11	Acanthe	Rose Layette	44	Blue Jeans	Light Green
12	Spring Rose	Cerise	45	Rose Layette	Malva
13	Spring Rose	Cerise	46	Blue Layette	Glacier
14	Rose Layette	Rose Soraya	47	Blue Layette	Glacier
15	Rose Layette	Rose Soraya	48	Amaranto	Jade
16	Rose Layette	Rose Soraya	49	Spring Rose	Ivory
17	Amaranto	Malva	50	Acanthe	Amaranto
18	Blue Jeans	Glacier	51	Turquoise	Spring Rose
19	Star Light	Light Green	52	Rose Layette	Rose Layette
20	Turquoise	Rose Layette	53	Rose Layette	Rose Layette
21	Turquoise	Rose Layette	54	Amaranto	Cerise
22	Acanthe	Spring Rose	55	Blue Jeans	Rose Soraya
23	Amaranto	Amaranto	56	Blue Layette	Malva
24	Rose Layette	Cerise	57	Glacier	Jade
25	Spring Rose	Rose Soraya	58	Glacier	Jade
26	Acanthe	Malva	59	Aguamarina	Light Green
27	Glacier	Glacier	60	Blue Jeans	Amaranto
28	Glacier	Glacier	61	Blue Jeans	Amaranto
29	Aguamarina	Light Green	62	Blue Jeans	Amaranto
30	Aguamarina	Light Green	63	Star Light	Cerise
31	Star Light	Jade	64	Star Light	Cerise
32	Star Light	Jade	65	Star Light	Cerise
33	Blue Jeans	Spring Rose	66	Aguamarina	Rose Soraya
			67	Star Light	Cerise

BLANKET

Follow Chart for Color Changes each Round.

ROUND 1: *(Right Side)* Starting with first color, ch 4; join to first ch to form ring; ch 4 (counts as first tr, now and throughout), tr in ring, ch 4, [2 tr in ring ch 4] 5 times; join to first tr *(4th ch of beg ch-4)*. (12 tr & 6 ch-4 sps) Fasten off.

ROUND 2: Join next color with sl st to any ch-4 sp, ch 3 *(counts as first dc, now and throughout)*, 4 dc in same sp, ch 2, [5 dc in next ch-4 sp, ch 2] around; join to first dc (3rd ch of beg ch-3). (30 dc & 6 ch-2 sps) Fasten off.

ROUND 3: Using next color, **join with sc** *(see Special Stitches)* to first dc of any 5-dc group, sc in each of next 4 dc, 3 sc in next ch-2 sp, [sc in each of next 5 dc, 3 sc in next ch-2 sp] around; join to first sc. (48 sc)

ROUND 4: Ch 1, sc in same st as joining, sc in next sc, [pc (see Special Stitches) in next sc, sc in each of next 3 sc] around, ending with sc in last sc; join to first sc. (36 sc & 12 popcorns) Fasten off.

ROUND 5: Join next color with sl st to any popcorn, ch 3, dc in same st as joining, dc in each of next 3 sc, [2 dc in next pc, dc in each of next 3 sc] around; join to first dc (3rd ch of beg ch-3). (60 dc) Fasten off.

ROUND 6: Using next color, join with sc to first dc of any 2-dc group, [sc in next dc] around; join to first sc. (60 sc)

ROUND 7: Ch 1, sc in same st as joining, ch 2, skip next sc, [sc in next sc, ch 2, skip next sc] around; join to first sc. (30 sc & 30 ch-2 sps)

ROUND 8: Sl st in next ch-2 sp, ch 3, 2 dc in same sp, [3 dc in next ch-2 sp] around; join to first dc (3rd ch of beg ch-3). (90 dc) Fasten off.

ROUND 9: Using next color, join with sc to first dc of any 3-dc group, sc in each of next 2 dc, **FPtr** *(see Special Stitches)* around corresponding sc on Rnd 7, [sc in each of next 3 dc, **FPtr** around next sc on Rnd 7] around; join to first sc. (90 sc & 30 tr) Fasten off.

Hint: It may seem a little "ruffly" after this round but it will work out nicely in later rounds.

ROUND 10: Using next color, join with sc, to any first sc of 3-sc group, sc in each of next 2 sc, pc in next tr, [sc in each of next 3 sc, pc in next tr] around; join to first sc. (90 sc & 30 popcorns) Fasten off.

ROUND 11: Join next color with sl st to center sc of any 3-sc group, **beg-tr4-bob** *(see Special Stitches)* in same sc, ch 4, skip next 3 sts (sc, pc, sc), ***tr4-bob** *(see Special Stitches)* in next (center) sc, ch 4, skip next 3 sts; rep from * around; join to first tr. (30 bobbles & 30 ch-4 sps) Fasten off.

ROUND 12: Using next color, join with sc to any ch-4 sp, 4 sc in same sp, [5 sc in next ch-4 sp] around; join to first sc. (150 sc)

ROUND 13: Ch 3, [dc in next sc] around; join to first dc (3rd ch of beg ch-3). (150 dc) Fasten off.

ROUND 14: Using next color, join with sc to first dc, [sc in next dc] around; join to first sc. (150 sc)

ROUND 15: Ch 8 *(counts as first dc & ch-5)*, dc in same st as joining, skip next 4 sc, [(dc, ch 5, dc) in next sc, skip next 4 sc] around; join to first dc *(3rd ch of beg ch-8)* (60 dc & 30 ch-5 lps)

ROUND 16: Sl st in next ch-5 lp, ch 3, 6 dc in same sp, skip next dc, sc in sp between 2-dc, skip next dc, [7 dc in next ch-5 lp, sc in sp between 2-dc] around; join to first dc (3rd ch of beg ch-3). (210 dc & 30 sc) Fasten off.

ROUND 17: Using next color, join with sc to 4th *(center)* dc of any 7-dc group, ch 4, sc in same st as joining, *ch 3, skip next 3 dc, sl st in back loop of next sc, ch 3, skip next 3 dc**, (sc, ch 4, sc) in next *(center)* dc; rep from * around, ending at ** on final repeat; join to first sc. (60 sc, 30 ch-4 lps, 60 ch-3 lps & 30 sl sts) Fasten off.

ROUND 18: Join next color with sl st to any ch-4 lp, ch 3, (2 dc, [ch 4, 3 dc] twice) in same lp, *(3 dc, [ch 4, 3 dc] twice) in next ch-4 lp; rep from * around; join to first dc *(3rd ch of beg ch-3)*. (270 dc & 60 ch-4 lps) Fasten off.

ROUND 19: Join next color with sl st to first ch-4 lp made, ch 3, dc in same lp, [dc in each of next 3 dc, 2 dc in each of next 2 ch-4 lps] around, ending dc in each of next 3 dc, 2 dc in last ch-4 lp; join to first dc (3rd ch of beg ch-3). (210 dc) Fasten off.

ROUND 20: Join next color with sl st to sp between dc-groups, ch 4, 2 tr in same sp, *skip next 3 dc, (tr, ch 3, tr) in next (center) dc, skip next 3 dc**, 3 tr in sp between dc-groups; rep from * around, ending at ** on final repeat; join to first tr (4th ch of beg ch-4). (30 groups of 3-tr, 60 tr & 30 ch-3 sps)

ROUND 21: Ch 3, dc in each of next 3 tr, [2 dc in next ch-3 sp, dc in each of next 5 tr] around, ending, 2 dc in next ch-3 sp, dc in last tr; join to first dc (3rd ch of beg ch-3). (210 dc) Fasten off.

ROUND 22: Using next color, join with sc to second dc (made in center tr of 3-tr group), working in Rnd 20, skip next tr (of 3-tr group), *FPtr in next tr, working in current Rnd, sc in each of next 6 dc, working in Rnd 20, FPtr in next tr**, working in current Rnd, sc in next dc (above center tr of 3-tr group), working in Rnd 20, skip next 3-tr group; rep from * around, ending at ** on final repeat; join to first sc. (210 sc & 60 tr) Fasten off.

ROUND 23: Join next color with sl st to first tr, ch 3, dc in each of next 8 sts, ch 3, [dc in each of next 9 sts, ch 3] around; join to first dc (3rd ch of beg ch-3). (270 dc & 30 ch-3 lps) Fasten off.

ROUND 24: Join next color with sl st to any ch-3 lp, ch 5 (counts as first tr & ch-1), (tr2-bob (see Special Stitches), ch 3, tr2-bob, ch 1, tr) in same lp, *ch 1, skip next 4 dc, sc in next dc, ch 1, skip next 4 dc**, (tr, ch 1, tr2-bob, ch 3, tr2-bob, ch 1, tr) in next ch-3 lp; rep from * around, ending at ** on final repeat; join to first tr (4th ch of beg ch-5). (60 tr, 60 tr-bobbles, 30 sc, 120 ch-1 sps & 30 ch-3 sps) Fasten off.

ROUND 25: Using next color, join with sc to any ch-3 sp, (sc, ch 1, 2 sc) in same sp, *sc in next bob, sc in next ch-1 sp, sc in next tr, **sc2tog** (see Special Stitches) (using each of next 2 ch-1 sps – skipping sc), sc in next tr, sc in next ch-1 sp, sc in next bob**, (2 sc, ch 1, 2 sc) in next ch-3 sp; rep from * around, ending at ** on final repeat; join to first sc. (330 sc & 30 ch-1 sps) Fasten off.

ROUND 26: Using next color, join with sc to any ch-1 sp, sc in same sp, *skip next sc, hdc in next sc, dc in next sc, tr in next sc, **tr3tog** (see Special Stitches) (over next 3 sc), tr in next sc, dc in next sc, hdc in next sc, skip next sc**, 2 sc in next ch-1 sp; rep from * around, ending at **

on final repeat; join to first sc. (60 sc, 60 hdc, 60 dc & 90 tr) Fasten off.

ROUND 27: Using next color, join with sc to first sc of any 2-sc group, sc in each of next 4 sts, [2 sc in next tr, sc in each of next 8 sts] around, ending 2 sc in next tr, sc in each of next 3 sts; join to first sc. (300 sc)

ROUND 28: Ch 1, sc in same st as joining, [pc in next sc, sc in each of next 9 sc] around, ending pc in next sc, sc in each of next 8 sc; join to first sc. (270 sc & 30 popcorns) Fasten off.

ROUND 29: Using next color, join with sc to any pc, ch 2, skip next sc, [sc in next st, ch 2, skip next sc] around; join to first sc. (150 sc & 150 ch-2 sps)

ROUND 30: Sl st in next ch-2 sp, ch 3, dc in same sp, [2 dc in next ch-2 sp] around; join to first dc (3rd ch of beg ch-3). (300 dc) Fasten off.

ROUND 31: Using next color, join with sl st around back post of first dc (ch-3), ch 3, [BPdc (see Special Stitches) in next dc] around; join to first dc (3rd ch of beg ch-3). (300 dc)

ROUND 32: Ch 1, sc in same st as joining, [sc in next dc] around; join to first sc. (300 sc) Fasten off.

ROUND 33: Using next color, join with sl st to first sc, ch 2, 2 hdc in same st as joining, hdc in each of next 4 sc, [2 hdc in next sc, hdc in each of next 4 sc] around; join to first hdc. (360 hdc) Fasten off.

Squaring the Circle

ROUND 34: Join next color with sl st to first hdc, ch 5 (counts as first dtr), 2 **dtr** (see Special Stitches) in same hdc, ch 2, 3 dtr in next hdc, *skip next hdc, tr in each of next 9 hdc, dc in each of next 13 hdc, hdc in each of next 6 hdc, sc in each of next 30 hdc, hdc, in each of next 6 hdc, dc in each of next 13 hdc, tr in each of next 9 hdc, skip next hdc*, 3 dtr in next hdc, ch 2, 3 dtr in next hdc; rep from * around, ending at ** on final repeat; join to first dtr (5th ch of beg ch-5). (24 dtr, 72 tr, 104 dc, 48 hdc, 120 sc & 4 ch-2 sps) Fasten off.

ROUND 35: Join next color with sl st to any ch-2 sp, ch 5 (counts as first tr & ch-1), (tr2-bob, ch 3, tr2-bob, ch 1, tr) in same sp, *skip next 3 dtr, dc in each of next 14 sts, hdc in each of next 6 sts, sc in each of next 46 sts, hdc in each of next 6 sts, dc in each of next 14 sts, skip next 3 sts**, (tr, ch 1, tr2-bob, ch 3, tr2-bob, ch 1, tr) in next ch-2 sp; rep from * around, ending at ** on final repeat; join to first tr (4th ch of beg ch-5). (16 tr, 112 dc. 48 hdc, 184 sc, 8 ch-1 sps & 4 ch-3 sps) Fasten off.

ROUND 36: Join next color with sl st to any ch-3 sp, ch 4, (3 tr, **p3** (see Special Stitches), 4 tr) in same sp, *skip next tr, sc in next ch-1 sp, skip next tr, 5 tr in sp before next dc, skip next 2 dc, hdc in next dc, working in Rnd 34, FPtr in first tr after 3 dtr-groups, hdc in each of next 12 sts, sc in each of next 56 sts, hdc in each of next 12 sts, working in Rnd 34, FPtr in last tr before 3 dtr-groups, hdc in next dc, skip next 2 dc, 5 tr in sp before next tr, skip next tr, sc in next ch-1 sp, skip next tr**, (4 tr, p3, 4 tr) in next ch-3 sp; rep from * around, ending at ** on final repeat; join to first tr 4 (4th ch of beg ch-4). (80 tr, 104 hdc, 232 sc & 4 picots) Fasten off.

Note: When working in the back loops, I suggest working through the back loop together with the loop below the back loop (third loop). This makes the stitch more stable and doesn't leave any holes.

ROUND 37: Join next color with sl st to any picot, ch 5 (counts as first dc & ch-2), (pc, ch 2, dc) in same picot, *ch 2, skip next 2 tr, pc in next tr, ch 2, skip next 4 sts, pc in next (center) tr, ch 4, skip next 6 sts, pc in next hdc, working in **back loops** only, dc in each of next 12 sts, hdc in each of next 5 sts, sc in each of next 40 sts, hdc in each of next 5 sts, dc in each of next 12 sts, working in **both loops**, pc in next hdc, ch 4, skip next 6 sts, pc in next (center) tr, ch 2, skip next 4 sts, pc in next tr, ch 2, skip next 2 tr**, (dc, ch 2, pc, ch 2, dc) in next picot; rep from * around, ending at ** on final repeat; join to first dc (3rd ch of beg ch-5) (28 popcorn, 104 dc, 40 hdc, 160 sc, 24 ch-2 sps, 8 ch-4 sps &) Fasten off.

ROUND 38: Join next color with sl st to corner popcorn, ch 6 (counts as first tr & ch 2), tr in same pc, *2 tr in next ch-2 sp, skip next dc, 3 tr in each of next 2 ch-2 sps (skipping pc), skip next pc, 5 tr in next ch-4 sp, skip next pc, working in back loops only, dc in each of next 2 sts, hdc in each of next 9 sts, sc in each of next 52 sts, hdc in each of next 9 sts, dc in each of next 2 sts, skip pc, 5 tr in

next ch-4 sp, skip pc, 3 tr in each of next 2 ch-2 sps, skip next pc, 2 tr in next ch-2 sp**, (tr, ch 2, tr) in next pc; rep from * around, ending at ** on final repeat; join to first tr (4th ch of beg ch-6). (112 tr, 16 dc, 72 hdc, 208 sc & 4 ch-2 sps) Fasten off.

ROUND 39: Join next color with sl st to any corner ch-2 sp, ch 6 (counts as first tr & ch-2), 2 tr in same sp, *BPtr (see Special Stitches) in each of next 15 sts, dc in each of next 2 sts, hdc in each of next 2 hdc, sc in each of next 64 sts, hdc in each of next 2 hdc, dc in each of next 2 sts, BPtr in each of next 15 sts**, (2 tr, ch 2, 2 tr) in next corner ch-2 sp; rep from * around, ending at ** on final repeat, tr in same first corner sp; join to first tr (4th ch of beg ch-6). (136 tr, 16 dc, 16 hdc, 256 sc & 4 corner ch-2 sps)

Note: From Rounds 40 to 49, unless mentioned otherwise, when working in stitches (not spaces), work in the back loops only.

ROUND 40: Ch 1, *(sc, ch 2, sc) in next corner ch-2 sp, working in **back loops** only, sc in each of next 17 sts, hdc in each of next 20 sts, sc in each of next 32 sts, hdc in next of next 20 sts, sc in each of next 17 sts; rep from * around; join to first sc. (160 hdc, 272 sc & 4 corner ch-2 sps) Fasten off.

ROUND 41: Using next color, join with sc to any corner ch-2 sp, ch 2, sc in same sp, *working in **back loops** only, sc in each of next 19 sts, [dc in **front loop** of corresponding st on Rnd 39, working in back loops on current rnd, sc in each of next 2 sts] 24 times, sc in each of next 17 sts**, (sc, ch 2, sc) in next corner ch-2 sp; rep from * around, ending at ** on final repeat; join to first sc. (344 sc, 96 dc & 4 corner ch-2 sps) Fasten off.

ROUND 42: Using next color, join with sc to any corner ch-2 sp, ch 2, sc in same sp, *working in **back loops** only, sc in each of next 21 sts, [dc in **front loop** of corresponding st on Rnd 40, working in **back loops** on current rnd, sc in each of next 2 sts] 24 times, sc in each of next 19 sts**, (sc, ch 2, sc) in next corner ch-2 sp; rep from * around, ending at ** on final repeat; join to first sc. (352 sc, 96 dc & 4 corner ch-2 sps) Fasten off.

ROUND 43: Join next color with sl st to any corner ch-2 sp, ch 5 (counts as first dc & ch-2, now and throughout),

dc in same sp, *working in **back loops** only, dc in each of next 112 sts**, (dc, ch 2, dc) in next corner ch-2 sp; rep from * around, ending at ** on final repeat; join to first dc *(3rd ch of beg ch-5)*. (456 dc & 4 corner ch-2 sps) Fasten off.

ROUND 44: Join next color with sl st to any corner ch-2 sp, ch 5, dc in same sp, *working in **back loops only**, dc in each of next 2 dc, skip next 2 dc, [**v2-st** *(see Special Stitches)* in next dc, skip next 2 dc] 36 times, dc in each of next 2 dc**, (dc, ch 2, dc) in next corner ch-2 sp; rep from * around, ending at ** on final repeat; join to first dc *(3rd ch of beg ch-5)*. (24 dc, 144 v-stitches & 4 corner ch-2 sps) Fasten off.

ROUND 45: Using next color, join with sc to any corner ch-2 sp, ch 2, sc in same sp, *working in **back loops** only, sc in each of next 3 dc, [sc in sp before next v-st, pc in next v-st] 36 times, sc in sp after last v-st, sc in each of next 3 sc**, (sc, ch 2, sc) in next corner ch-2 sp; rep from * around, ending at ** on final repeat; join to first sc. (144 popcorn, 180 sc & 4 corner ch-2 sps). Fasten off.

ROUND 46: Join next color with sl st to any corner ch-2 sp, ch 5, dc in same sp, *working in **back loops** only, dc in each of next 5 sc, [ch 2, skip pc, dc in next sc] 36 times, dc in each of next 4 sc**, (dc, ch 2, dc) in next corner ch-2 sp; rep from * around, ending at ** on final repeat; join to first dc (3rd ch of beg ch-5). (188 dc, 144 ch-2 sps & 4 corner ch-2 sps)

ROUND 47: Sl st in next corner ch-2 sp, ch 6 (counts as first tr & ch-2), tr in same sp working in **back loops** only, *tr in each of next 119 sts (working in ch-sts not sps)**, (tr, ch 2, tr) in next corner ch-2 sp; rep from * around, ending at ** on final repeat; join to first tr (4th ch of beg ch-5). (484 tr & 4 corner ch-2 sps) Fasten off.

ROUND 48: Join next color with sl st to any corner ch-2 sp, ch 5, dc in same sp, *BPdc in each of next 121 tr**, (dc, ch 2, dc) in next corner ch-2 sp; rep from * around, ending at ** on final repeat; join to first dc *(3rd ch of beg ch-5)*. (492 dc & 4 corner ch-2 sps) Fasten off.

ROUND 49: Join next color with sc to any corner ch-2 sp, ch 2, (hdc, ch 2 hdc) in same sp, *working in **back loops** only, hdc in each of next 123 dc**, (hdc, ch 2, hdc) in next corner ch-2 sp; rep from * around, ending at ** on final repeat; join to first hdc. (500 hdc & 4 corner ch-2 sps) Fasten off.

ROUND 50: Join next color with sl st to any corner ch-2 sp, ch 8 (counts as first tr & ch-4, now and throughout), tr in same sp, *ch 1, skip next hdc, **tr3bob** *(see Special Stitches)* in next hdc, [ch 2, skip next 2 hdc, tr3bob in next hdc] across to next corner, ch 1**, (tr, ch 4, tr) in next corner ch-2 sp; rep from * around, ending at ** on final repeat; join to first tr *(4th ch of beg ch-8)*. (168 bobbles, 164 ch-2 sps, 8 ch-1 sps, 8 tr & 4 corner ch-4 sps) Fasten off.

ROUND 51: Join next color with sl st to any corner ch-4 sp, ch 3, (dc, ch 2, 2 dc) in same sp, *[skip next st, **v1-st** *(see Special Stitches)* in next ch-sp] across to next corner, skip next tr**, (2 dc, ch 2, 2 dc) in next corner ch-2 sp; rep from * around, ending at ** on final repeat; join to first dc *(3rd ch of beg ch-3)*. (16 dc, 172 v-sts & 4 corner ch-2 sps) Fasten off.

ROUND 52: Join next color with sl st to any corner ch-2 sp, ch 5, dc in same sp, *dc in each of next 2 dc, [**v3-st** *(see Special Stitches)* in next v-st, ch 2, skip next v-st] 21 times, v3-st in next v-st, dc in each of next 2 dc**, (dc, ch 2, dc) in corner ch-2 sp; rep from * around, ending at ** on final repeat; join to first dc *(3rd ch of beg ch-5)*. (24 dc, 88 v-sts, 84 ch-2 sps & 4 corner ch-2 sps)

ROUND 53: Ch 1, *(sc, ch 2, sc) in next corner ch-2 sp, sc in each of next 3 dc, 7 dc in v-st, [sc in next ch-2 sp, 7 dc in next v-st] 21 times, sc in each of next 3 dc; rep from * around; join to first sc. (116 sc, 88 dc-shells & 4 corner ch-2 sps) Fasten off.

ROUND 54: Using next color, join with sc to any corner ch-2 sp, ch 2, sc in same sp, *sc in each of next 3 sc, sl st in back loop of next sc, [ch 3, skip next 3 dc, (sc, ch 4, sc) in next (center) dc, ch 3, skip next 3 dc, sl st in back loop of next sc] 22 times, sc in each of next 3 sc**, (sc, ch 2, sc) in next corner ch-2 sp; rep from * around, ending at ** on final repeat; join to first sc. (208 sc, 176 ch-3 sps, 88 ch-4 lps, 92 sl sts & 4 corner ch-2 sps) Fasten off.

ROUND 55: Join next color with sl st to any corner ch-2 sp, ch 8, tr in same sp, tr in each of next 4 sc, *skip next ch-3 sp, (2 dc, ch 3, 3 dc, ch 3, 2 dc) in each of next 22 ch-4 lps (skipping ch-3 sps), tr in each of next 4 sc**, (tr, ch 4, tr) in next corner ch-2 sp; rep from * around, ending at ** on final repeat; join to first tr (4th ch of beg ch-8). (40 tr, 616 dc, 264 ch-3 sps & 4 corner ch-4 sps) Fasten off.

ROUND 56: Join next color with sl st to any corner ch-4 sp, ch 4, (tr, ch 4, 2 tr) in same sp, *tr in each of next 5 tr, [skip next 2 dc, 2 sc in next ch-3 sp, sc in each of next 3 dc, 2 sc in next ch-3 sp, skip next 2 dc] 22 times, tr in each of next 5 tr**, (tr, ch 4, tr) in next corner ch-4 sp;rep from * around, ending at ** on final repeat; join to first tr (4th ch of beg ch-8). (56 tr, 616 sc & 4 corner ch-4 sps) Fasten off.

ROUND 57: Join next color with sl st to any corner ch-4 sp, ch 6 (counts as first dc & ch-3, now and throughout), 2 dc in same sp, *dc in each of next 168 sts**, (2 dc, ch 3, 2 dc) in next corner ch-4 sp; rep from * around, ending at ** on final repeat, dc in first corner sp; join to first dc (3rd ch of beg ch-6). (688 dc & 4 corner ch-3 sps)

ROUND 58: Sl st in next ch-3 sp, ch 6, dc in same sp, *dc in each of next 172 dc**, (dc, ch 3, dc) in next corner ch-3 sp; rep from * around, ending at ** on final repeat, dc in first corner sp; join to first dc (3rd ch of beg ch-6). (696 dc & 4 corner ch-3 sps) Fasten off.

ROUND 59: Join next color with sl st to any corner ch-3 sp, ch 6, dc in same sp, *dc in each of next 174 sts**, (dc, ch 3, dc) in next corner ch-3 sp; join to first dc (3rd ch of beg ch-6). (704 dc & 4 corner ch-3 sps) Fasten off.

ROUND 60: Join next color with sl st to any corner ch-3 sp, ch 6, dc in same sp, *dc in each of next 5 dc, ch 2, skip next 2 dc, dc in next dc, [ch 2, skip next 2 dc, dc in each of next 2 dc, ch 2, skip next 2 dc, dc in next dc] 23 times, ch 2, skip next 2 dc, dc in each of next 5 dc**, (dc, ch 2, dc) in next corner ch-2 sp; rep from * around, ending at ** on final repeat. (328 dc, 192 ch-2 sps & 4 corner ch-2 sps)

ROUND 61: Sl st in next corner ch-2 sp, ch 6, dc in same sp, *dc in each of next 6 dc, [ch 3, skip ch-sp, sc in next dc, ch 3, skip ch-sp, dc in each of next 2 dc] 23 times, ch 3, skip ch-sp, sc in next dc, ch 3, skip ch-sp, dc in each of next 6 dc**, (dc, ch 3, dc) in next corner ch-2 sp; rep from * around, ending at ** on final repeat; join to first dc (3rd ch of beg ch-6). (240 dc, 96 sc, 192 ch-3 sps & 4 corner ch-3 sps)

ROUND 62: Sl st in next corner ch-3 sp, ch 6, dc in same sp, *dc in each of next 7 dc, [dc in each of next 2 ch (of ch-3), ch 2, skip next (ch, sc, ch), dc in each of next 2 ch, dc in each of next 2 dc] 24 times, dc in each of next 5 dc**, (dc, ch 3, dc) in next corner ch-3 sp; rep from * around, ending at ** on final repeat; join to first dc (3rd ch of beg ch-6). (632 dc, 96 ch-2 sps, & 4 corner ch-3 sps) Fasten off.

ROUND 63: Join next color with sl st to any corner ch-3 sp, ch 6, dc in same sp, *dc in each of next 206 sts (working in all ch-sts not sps)**, (dc, ch 3, dc) in next corner ch-3 sp; rep from * around, ending at ** on final repeat; join to first dc (3rd ch of beg ch-6). (832 dc & 4 corner ch-3 sps)

ROUND 64: Sl st in next ch-3 sp, ch 6, dc in same sp, *dc in next dc, [ch 2, skip next 2 dc, dc in next dc] 69 times**, (dc, ch 3, dc) in next corner ch-3 sp; rep from * around, ending at ** on final repeat; join to first dc (3rd ch of beg ch-6). (288 dc, 276 ch-2 sps & 4 corner ch-3 sps)

ROUND 65: Sl st in next ch 3 sp, ch 3, (dc, ch 2, 2 dc) in same sp, *dc in each of next 2 dc, 2 dc in next ch-sp, [ch 1, skip next dc, 2 dc in next ch-2 sp] 68 times, dc in next 2 dc**, (2 dc, ch 2, 2 dc) in next corner ch-3 sp; rep from * around, ending at ** on final repeat; join to first dc (3rd ch of beg ch-3). (584 dc, 272 ch-1 sps & 4 corner ch-2 sps) Fasten off.

ROUND 66: Using next color, join with sc to any corner ch-2 sp, ch 2, sc in same sp, *sc in each of next 6 dc, FPtr in corresponding dc of Rnd 64, [sc in each of next 2 dc, FPtr in corresponding dc of Rnd 64] 67 times, sc in each of next 6 dc**, (sc, ch 2, sc) in next corner ch-2 sp; rep from * around, ending at ** on final repeat; join to first sc. (592 sc, 272 tr & 4 corner ch-2 sps) Fasten off.

ROUND 67: Using next color, join with sc to any corner ch-2 sp, ch 2, sc in same sp, *sc in each of next 218 sts**, (sc, ch 2, sc) in next corner ch-2 sp; rep from * around, ending at ** on final repeat; join to first sc. (880 sc & 4 corner ch-2 sps) Fasten off.

TASSELS - Make 4

Cut a piece of cardboard 6" (15 cm) wide by 4" (10 cm) long.

Place a separate 12" (30 cm) strand of yarn across the cardboard. Wind yarn 50 times around length of cardboard over 12" (30 cm) strand.

Tie ends of 12" (30 cm) strand tightly together and remove cardboard. Do not trim the 12" (30 cm) strand (used for attaching to corners.

Using sharp scissors, cut yarn at opposite end.

Wrap another short piece of yarn tightly around all the strands a few times, about 1" (2.5 cm) below the top, securing ends with a knot. Trim ends of the tassel.

With right side of Blanket facing, using both ends of 12" (30 cm) strand and yarn needle, *insert needle from front to back through corner ch-2 sp, bring needle back through top of tassel (under knot); repeat from * until secure, ending at back of Blanket. Fasten off and weave in all ends.

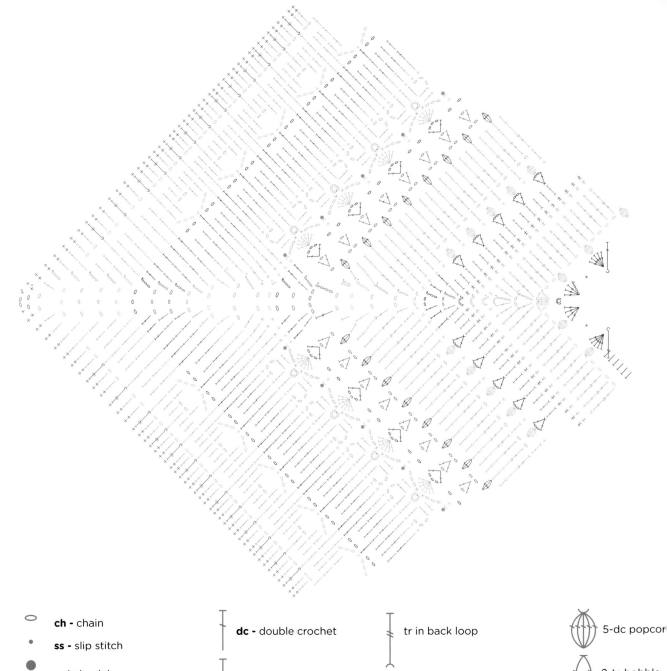

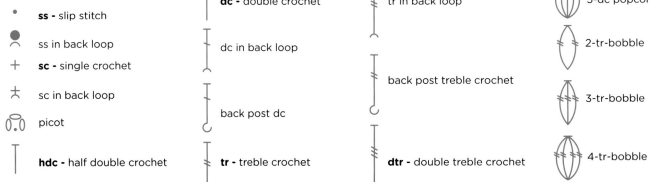

⬭ **ch -** chain	⊤ **dc -** double crochet	⊤ tr in back loop	🎈 5-dc popcorn
• **ss -** slip stitch			
● ss in back loop	⊤ dc in back loop		🔶 2-tr-bobble
+ **sc -** single crochet		back post treble crochet	
⊼ sc in back loop	⊤ back post dc		🔷 3-tr-bobble
0̸0 picot			
			🎈 4-tr-bobble
	hdc - half double crochet	**tr -** treble crochet	**dtr -** double treble crochet

24

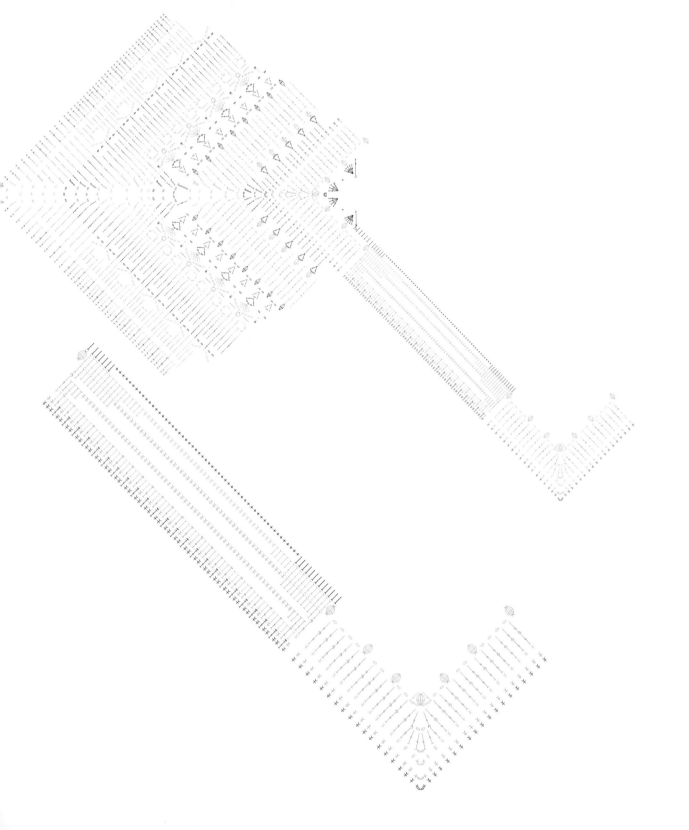

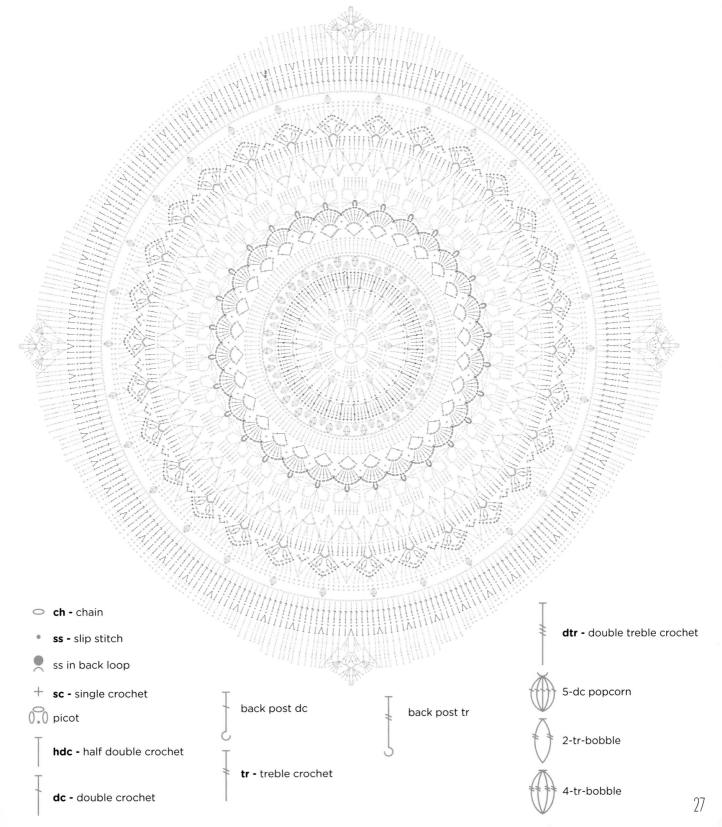

ch - chain

ss - slip stitch

ss in back loop

sc - single crochet

picot

hdc - half double crochet

dc - double crochet

back post dc

tr - treble crochet

back post tr

dtr - double treble crochet

5-dc popcorn

2-tr-bobble

4-tr-bobble

GARDEN ROWS CUSHION

The cat's out of the bag... This is my favorite cushion in the entire book! Creating it was a challenge, and after many, many frogging sessions, I reached perfection. It will come as no surprise that I used popcorns - my favorite stitch - in this design. As you can see, I used blended color tones again, and one can't stop looking at it!

This gorgeous design is one large square, which joins up beautifully at the back. Instead of crocheting the edges together, I opted for sewing (weaving) using two long lengths of chain stitches. This way, the cover can easily be removed for laundering. Who know, this might become your favorite cushion too.

Finished Size

To fit 16" (40 cm) square
pillow form

FINISHED SIZE/S

To fit 16" (40 cm) square pillow form

MATERIALS

DMC Natura Just Cotton

      Color A – Lobelia (#82)

      Color B – Spring Rose (#07)

      Color C – Amaranto (#33)

      Color D – Glacier (#87)

      Color E – Aguamarine (#25)

      Color F – Ibiza (#01)

One ball of each color makes one Cushion Cover.

Hook: Size E-4 (3.50 mm)

Scissors & Yarn Needle

16" (40 cm) square Pillow Form

PATTERN NOTES

1 A Magic Ring (see Techniques) can be used instead of the chain ring in Round 1.

2 All joins are slip stitches, unless otherwise indicated.

3 All new colors are joined with right side facing, unless otherwise indicated.

4 Weave in all ends as you go.

5 Standing stitches (see Techniques) can be used to start a round with a new color.

6 An invisible join (see Techniques) can be used at the end of a round to finish a color.

SPECIAL STITCHES

Back Post Double Crochet (BPdc): Yarn over hook, insert hook from back to front to back around post of indicated stitch, yarn over and draw up loop, [yarn over and pull through 2 loops] twice (double crochet made).

Popcorn (pc): Work 5 dc in same stitch or space indicated, drop lp from hook, insert hook from front to back in first dc made, pull dropped lp through, ch 1 (to lock).

Join With Single Crochet (join with sc): With slip knot on hook, insert hook into stitch or space indicated and pull up a loop (2 loops on hook). Yarn over and pull through both loops on hook (first single crochet made).

Back Post Half-Double Crochet (BPhdc): Yarn over hook, insert hook from back to front to back around post of indicated stitch, yarn over and draw up loop, yarn over and pull through all 3 loops on hook (half-double crochet made).

Front Post Double Crochet (FPdc): Yarn over hook, insert hook from front to back to front around post of indicated stitch, yarn over and draw up loop, [yarn over and pull through 2 loops] twice (double crochet made).

Front Post Half-Double Crochet (FPhdc): Yarn over hook, insert hook from front to back to front around post of indicated stitch, yarn over and draw up loop, yarn over and pull through all 3 loops on hook (half-double crochet made).

Treble Decrease (over 5 stitches) (tr3tog): Yarn over hook twice, insert hook in next stitch indicated and draw up a loop (4 loops on hook), [yarn over, pull through 2 loops on hook] twice (2 loops on remain on hook), *skip next st, yarn over hook twice, insert hook in next stitch and draw up a loop, [yarn over, pull through 2 loops on hook] twice; rep from * once more, yarn over, pull through all 4 loops on hook.

Single Crochet Decrease: (sc2tog): Insert hook in first stitch or space indicated and draw up a loop (2 loops on hook). Insert hook in next stitch or space indicated and draw up a loop (3 loops on hook). Yarn over and pull through all loops on hook.

Treble Decrease (over 2 stitches) (tr2tog): Yarn over hook twice, insert hook in stitch or space indicated and draw up a loop (4 loops on hook), [yarn over, pull through 2 loops on hook] twice (2 loops on remain on hook), yarn over hook twice, insert hook in next stitch or space and draw up a loop, [yarn over, pull through 2 loops on hook] twice (3 loops remain on hook), yarn over, pull through all 3 loops on hook.

CUSHION COVER

ROUND 1: *(Right Side)* Starting with Color A, ch 4; join to first ch to form ring; ch 4 (counts as first tr, now and throughout), 15 tr in ring; join to first tr (*4th ch of beg ch-4*). (16 tr) Fasten off.

ROUND 2: Join Color B with sl st around back post of any tr, ch 4 (counts as first dc & ch-1, now and throughout), [**BPdc** (*see Special Stitches*) in next tr, ch 1] around; join to first dc (*3rd ch of beg ch-4*). (16 dc & 16 ch-1 sps)

ROUND 3: Ch 1, [3 sc in next ch-1 sp] around; join to first sc. (48 sc) Fasten off Color B.

ROUND 4: Join Color C with sl st to first sc of any 3-sc group, ch 3 (counts as first dc, now and throughout), **pc** (*see Special Stitches*) in next sc, dc in next sc, ch 1, [dc in next sc, pc in next sc, dc in next sc, ch 1] around; join to first dc (*3rd ch of beg ch-3*). (32 dc, 16 popcorns & 16 ch-1 sps) Fasten off Color C.

ROUND 5: Using Color D, **join with sc** (*see Special Stitches*) in any ch-1 sp, *sc in each of next 3 sts, ch 2, skip next ch-1 sp, sc in each of next 3 sts**, sc in next ch-1 sp; rep from * around, ending at ** on final repeat; join to first sc. (56 sc & 8 ch-2 sps)

ROUND 6: Using Color E, join with sc to center sc of any 7-sc group, *ch 2, skip next 3 sc, (2 dc, ch 3, 2 dc) in next ch-2 sp, ch 2, skip next 3 sc**, sc in next sc; rep from * around, ending at ** on final repeat; join to first sc. (8 sc, 8 shells & 16 ch-2 sps)

ROUND 7: Ch 1, sc in same st as joining, *ch 1, dc in each of next 2 dc, 8 dc in next ch-3 sp, dc in each of next 2 dc, ch 1**, sc in next sc; rep from * around, ending at ** on final repeat; join to first sc. (8 x 12-dc shells, 8 sc & 16 ch-1 sps) Fasten off Color E.

ROUND 8: Join Color D with sl st around back post of first dc in any shell, ch 2, **BPhdc** (*see Special Stitches*) in same st, BPhdc in each of next 5 dc, ch 2, BPhdc in each of next 6 dc, **FPdc** (*see Special Stitches*) in corresponding sc on Rnd 6, *BPhdc in each of next 6 dc, ch 2, BPhdc in each of next 6 dc, FPdc in corresponding sc on Rnd 6; rep from * around; join to first hdc. (96 hdc, 8dc & 8 ch-2 sps) Fasten off Color D.

ROUND 9: Using Color F, join with sc to any ch-2 sp, 2 sc in same sp, *skip next hdc, working in **back loops** only, hdc in next hdc, dc in next hdc, 2 dc in next hdc, **tr3tog** (*see Special Stitches*) over next 5 sts, 2 dc in next hdc, dc in next hdc, hdc in next hdc, skip next hdc**, 3 sc in next ch-2 sp; rep from * around, ending at ** on final repeat; join to first sc. (24 sc, 16 hdc, 48 dc & 8 tr)

ROUND 10: Ch 1, sc in same st as joining, sc in each of next 6 sts, [3 sc in next tr, sc in each of next 11 sts] around, ending 3 sc in next tr, sc in each of next 4 sts; join to first sc. (112 sc)

ROUND 11: Ch 3, [dc in next sc] around; join to first dc (*3rd ch of beg ch-3*). (112 dc) Fasten off Color F.

ROUND 12: Using Color C, join with sc to third dc, dc in each of next 5 dc, [2 sc in next dc, sc in each of next 6 sc] around, ending with 2 sc in last dc; join to first sc. (128 sc) Fasten off Color C.

ROUND 13: Join Color B with sl st to first sc, ch 3, [dc in next sc] around; join to first dc (**3rd ch of beg ch-3**). (128 dc) Fasten off Color B.

ROUND 14: Using Color A, join with sc to first dc, sc in each of next 6 dc, *ch 2, skip next dc, sc in each of next 7 dc**, ch 4, skip next dc, sc in each of next 7 dc; rep from * around, ending with ch 1, skip next dc, join with dc to first sc (*to form last ch-4 loop and position yarn for next round*). (112 sc, 8 ch-2 sps & 8 ch-4 lps)

ROUND 15: Beg-tr-cl (*see Special Stitches*) in loop under hook, ch 3, **tr-cl** (*see Special Stitches*) in same lp, *ch 4, skip next 3 sc, sc in next sc, ch 3, skip next 3 sc, 3 dc in next ch-2 sp, ch 3, skip next 3 sc, sc in next sc, ch 4, skip next 3 sc**, (tr-cl, ch 3, tr-cl) in next ch-4 sp; rep from * around, ending at ** on final repeat; join to first tr. (16 cl, 8 shells, 16 sc, 16 ch-3 sps & 16 ch-4 lps) Fasten off Color A.

ROUND 16: Join Color E with sl st to any ch-3 sp between 2 clusters, ch 3, 4 dc in same sp, *sc in next tr, 6 dc in next ch-4 lp, skip next sc, 2 hdc in next ch-3 sp, skip next dc, 3 sc in next (center) dc, skip next dc, 2 hdc in next ch-3 sp, skip next sc, 6 dc in next ch-4 lp, sc in next tr**, 5 dc in next ch-3 sp; rep from * around, ending at ** on final repeat. (136 dc, 32 hdc & 40 sc) Fasten off Color E.

ROUND 17: Using Color D, join with sc to center dc of any 5-dc group, sc in same st, *sc in each of next 2 dc, skip next sc, BPdc in each of next 6 dc, dc in each of next 3 sts, skip next (center) sc, dc in each of next 3 sts, BPdc in each of next 6 dc, skip next sc, sc in each of next 2 dc**, 2 sc in next (center) dc; rep from * around, ending at ** on final repeat. (144 dc & 48 sc) Fasten off Color D.

ROUND 18: Using Color F, join with sc to first sc of any 2-sc group, *ch 1, sc in each of next 3 sc, **sc2tog** (see Special Stitches) using next 2 dc, [sc in each of next 6 dc, sc2tog (using next 2 dc)] twice, sc in each of next 3 sc; rep from * around omitting last sc on final repeat; join to first sc. (168 sc & 8 ch-1 sps)

ROUND 19: Sl st in next ch-1 sp, ch 4, dc in same sp, dc in each of next 21 sc, [(dc, ch 1, dc) in next ch-1 sp, dc in each of next 21 sc] around; join to first dc (3rd ch of beg ch-3). (184 dc & 8 ch-1 sps)

ROUND 20: Ch 1, [(sc, ch 1, sc) in next ch-1 sp, sc in each of next 23 dc] around; join to first sc. (200 sc & 8 ch-1 sps) Fasten off Color F.

ROUND 21: Using Color C, join with sc to first sc, *sc in next ch-1 sp, sc in each of next 25 sc, sc in next ch-1 sp, sc in next sc, dc in each of next 3 sc, [pc in next sc, dc in each of next 3 sc] 5 times**, sc in next sc; rep from * around; join to first sc. (116 sc, 72 dc & 20 popcorns) Fasten off Color C.

ROUND 22: Using Color B with sc to any last dc (before sc), *sc in each of next 29 sc, (sc, dc) in next dc, dc in each of next 4 dc, [pc in next dc, dc in each of next 3 dc] 4 times, dc in next dc**, (dc, sc) in next dc; rep from * around, ending at ** on final repeat, dc in same st as first sc; join to first sc. (124 sc, 76 dc & 16 popcorns) Fasten off Color B.

ROUND 23: Using Color A, join with sc to any last dc (before sc), *sc in each of next 33 sc, (sc, dc) in next dc, dc in each of next 5 dc, [pc in next dc, dc in each of next 3 dc] 3 times, dc in each of next 2 dc**, (dc, sc) in next dc; rep from * around, ending at ** on final repeat, dc in same st as first sc; join to first sc. (140 sc, 72 dc & 12 popcorns) Fasten off Color A.

ROUND 24: Using Color E, join with sc to any last dc (before sc), *sc in each of next 37 sc, (sc, dc) in next dc, dc in each of next 6 dc, [pc in next dc, dc in each of next 3 dc] twice, dc in each of next 3 dc**, (dc, sc) in next dc; rep from * around, ending at ** on final repeat, dc in same st as first sc; join to first sc. (156 sc, 68 dc & 8 popcorns) Fasten off Color E.

ROUND 25: Using Color D, join with sc to any last dc (before sc), *sc in each of next 41 sc, (sc, dc) in next dc, dc in each of next 7 dc, pc in next dc, dc in each of next 7 dc **, (dc, sc) in next dc; rep from * around, ending at ** on final repeat, dc in same st as first sc; join to first sc. (172 sc, 64 dc & 4 popcorns) Fasten off Color D.

ROUND 26: Using Color C, join with sc to any last dc (before sc), *sc in each of next 45 sc, (sc, dc) in next dc, dc in each of next 2 dc, pc in next dc, dc in each of next 7 dc, pc in next dc, dc in each of next 2 dc**, (dc, sc) in next dc; rep from * around, ending at ** on final repeat, dc in same st as first sc; join to first sc. (188 sc, 52 dc & 8 popcorns) Fasten off Color C.

ROUND 27: Using Color B, join with sc to any last dc (before sc), *sc in each of next 49 sc, (sc, dc) in next dc, dc in each of next 2 dc, pc in next dc, dc in each of next 5 dc, pc in next dc, dc in each of next 2 dc**, (dc, sc) in next dc; rep from * around, ending at ** on final repeat, dc in same st as first sc; join to first sc. (204 sc, 44 dc & 8 popcorns) Fasten off Color B.

ROUND 28: Using Color A, join with sc to any last dc *(before sc)*, *sc in each of next 53 sc, (sc, dc) in next dc, dc in each of next 2 dc, pc in next dc, dc in each of next 3 dc, pc in next dc, dc in each of next 2 dc**, (dc, sc) in next dc; rep from * around, ending at ** on final repeat, dc in same st as first sc; join to first sc. (220 sc, 36 dc & 8 popcorns) Fasten off Color A.

ROUND 29: Using Color E, join with sc to any last dc *(before sc)*, *sc in each of next 57 sc, (sc, dc) in next dc, dc in each of next 2 dc, pc in next dc, dc in next dc, pc in next dc, dc in each of next 2 dc**, (dc, sc) in next dc; rep from * around, ending at ** on final repeat, dc in same st as first sc; join to first sc. (236 sc, 28 dc & 8 popcorns) Fasten off Color E.

ROUND 30: Using Color D, join with sc to any last dc *(before sc)*, *sc in each of next 61 sc, (sc, dc) in next dc, dc in each of next 2 dc, pc in next dc, dc in each of next 2 dc**, (dc, sc) in next dc; rep from * around, ending at ** on final repeat, dc in same st as first sc; join to first sc. (252 sc, 20 dc & 4 popcorns) Fasten off Color D.

ROUND 31: Using Color F, join with sc to any last dc *(before sc),* *sc in each of next 65 sc, (sc, dc) in next dc, ch 1, **tr2tog** *(see Special Stitches) (using next dc & pc)*, ch 3, tr2tog *(using same pc & next dc)*, ch 1**, (dc, sc) in next dc; rep from * around, ending at ** on final repeat, dc in same st as first sc; join to first sc. (268 sc, 8 tr, 8 dc, 8 ch-1 sps & 4 ch-3 sps) Fasten off Color F.

ROUND 32: Join Color F *(same as Rnd 31)* with sl st to any ch-3 sp, ch 5 *(counts as first dc & ch-2, now and throughout)*, 2 dc in same sp, *dc in next tr, dc in next ch-1 sp, dc in each of next 69 sts, dc in next ch-1 sp, dc in next tr**, (2 dc, ch 2, 2 dc) in next ch-3 sp; rep from * around, ending at ** on final repeat, dc in first ch-3 sp; join to first dc *(3rd ch of beg ch-5)*. (308 dc & 4 corner ch-2 sps)

ROUND 33: Sl st in next ch-2 sp, ch 5, 2 dc in same sp, *dc in each of next 77 dc **, (2 dc, ch 2, 2 dc) in next corner ch-2 sp; rep from * around, ending at ** on final repeat, dc in first ch-2 sp; join to first dc *(3rd ch of beg ch-5)*. (324 dc & 4 corner ch-2 sps)

ROUND 34: Ch 1, [(sc, ch 2, sc) in next ch-2 sp, sc in each of next 81 dc] around; join to first sc. (332 sc & 4 corner ch-2 sps). Fasten off Color F.

ROUND 35: Using Color A, join with sc to sp before first sc *(before ch-2 sp)*, *ch 4, skip next (sc, ch-2 sp, sc), *[sc in sp between sts, ch 3, skip next 3 sc] 27 times**, sc in sp between sts; rep from * around, ending at ** on final repeat; join to first sc. (28 sc & 27 ch-3 sps between corners & 4 corner ch-4 sps)

ROUND 36: Sl st in next ch-4 sp, ch 3, (2 dc, ch 2, 3 dc) in same sp, [3 dc in next ch-3 sp] around, working (3 dc, ch 2, 3 dc) in each corner ch-4 sp; join to first dc *(3rd ch of beg ch-3)*. (29 groups of 3-dc between corners & 4 corner ch-2 sps) Fasten off Color A.

ROUND 37: Using Color B, join with sc to any ch-2 sp, ch 3, sc in same sp, *[ch 3, skip next 3 dc, sc in sp between sts] 28 times, ch 3, skip next 3 dc**, (sc, ch 3, sc) in next corner ch-2 sp; rep from * around, ending at ** on final repeat; join to first sc. (30 sc & 29 ch-3 sps between corners & 4 corner ch 3 sps)

ROUND 38: Continuing with Color B, rep Rnd 36. (31 groups of 3-dc between corners & 4 corner ch-2 sps) Fasten off Color B.

ROUND 39: Using Color C, join with sc to any ch-2 sp, ch 3, sc in same sp, *[ch 3, skip next 3 dc, sc in sp between sts] 30 times, ch 3, skip next 3 dc**, (sc, ch 3, sc) in next corner ch-2 sp; rep from * around, ending at ** on final repeat; join to first sc. (32 sc & 31 ch-3 sps between corners & 4 corner ch-3 sps)

ROUND 40: Continuing with Color C, rep Rnd 36. (33 groups of 3-dc between corners & 4 corner ch-2 sps) Fasten off Color C.

ROUND 41: Using Color D, join with sc to any ch-2 sp, ch 3, sc in same sp, *[ch 3, skip next 3 dc, sc in sp between sts] 32 times, ch 3, skip next 3 dc**, (sc, ch 3, sc) in next corner ch-2 sp; rep from * around, ending at ** on final repeat; join to first sc. (34 sc & 33 ch-3 sps between corners & 4 corner ch-3 sps)

ROUND 42: Continuing with Color D, rep Rnd 36. (35 groups of 3-dc between corners & 4 corner ch-2 sps) Fasten off Color D.

ROUND 43: Using Color E, join with sc to any ch-2 sp, ch 3, sc in same sp, *[ch 3, skip next 3 dc, sc in sp between sts] 34 times, ch 3, skip next 3 dc**, (sc, ch 3, sc) in next corner ch-2 sp; rep from * around, ending at ** on final repeat; join to first sc. (36 sc & 35 ch-3 sps between corners & 4 corner ch-3 sps)

ROUND 44: Continuing with Color E, rep Rnd 36. (37 groups of 3-dc between corners & 4 corner ch-2 sps) Fasten off Color E.

ROUND 45: Using Color F, join with sc to any ch-2 sp, ch 3, sc in same sp, *[ch 3, skip next 3 dc, sc in sp between sts] 36 times, ch 3, skip next 3 dc**, (sc, ch 3, sc) in next corner ch-2 sp; rep from * around, ending at ** on final repeat; join to first sc. (38 sc & 37 ch-3 sps between corners & 4 corner ch-3 sps) Fasten off Color F.

TIES – Make 2

Using Color F, ch 250. Fasten off and weave in all ends.

ASSEMBLY – Use photo as guide

Place Cushion Cover face down (wrong side facing). Place pillow form in center of Cover, with each corner of pillow at center of each side of Cover. Fold adjacent corners over to meet at center. Using one Tie, insert through both corner ch-3 sps and pull both sides of Tie until of equal length.

Matching sts along each side, weave each length of Tie through the ch-3 sps. When you get to the corner of the Cushion Cover, weave Tie back towards center, creating 'cross-stitches'.

Insert other Tie in remaining 2 corner ch-3 sps, and repeat the weaving, ending with all four ends of Ties in the center. Either knot all ends together to create a tassel, or sew them in to hide them.

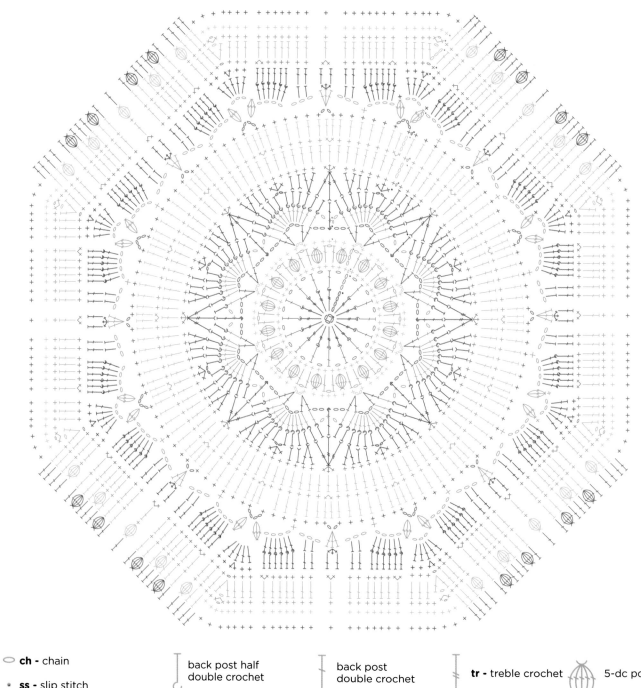

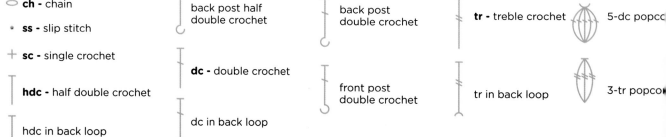

⬭ **ch -** chain

• **ss -** slip stitch

+ **sc -** single crochet

hdc - half double crochet

hdc in back loop

back post half double crochet

dc - double crochet

dc in back loop

back post double crochet

front post double crochet

tr - treble crochet

tr in back loop

5-dc popcc

3-tr popco

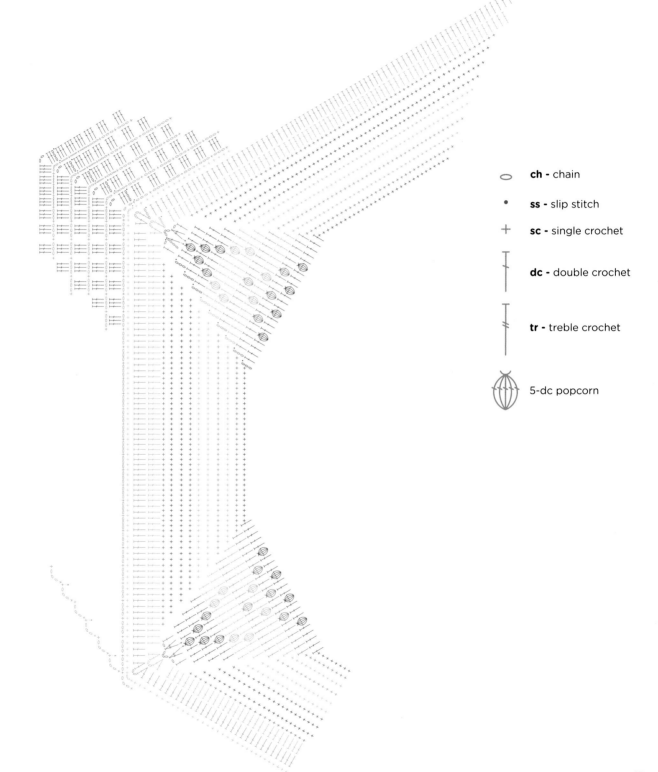

ch - chain

ss - slip stitch

sc - single crochet

dc - double crochet

tr - treble crochet

5-dc popcorn

SUNNY CITRUS CUSHION

When I was making the motifs for this cushion, I was constantly reminded of citrus fruits. Yep, in the yellow tones I used, they looked like slices of lemons. I was aiming for the sun, but citrus fruit was close enough. This cushion will add the warmth of the sunny day to any room. As a thought… More of these motifs joined together would make a lovely blanket.

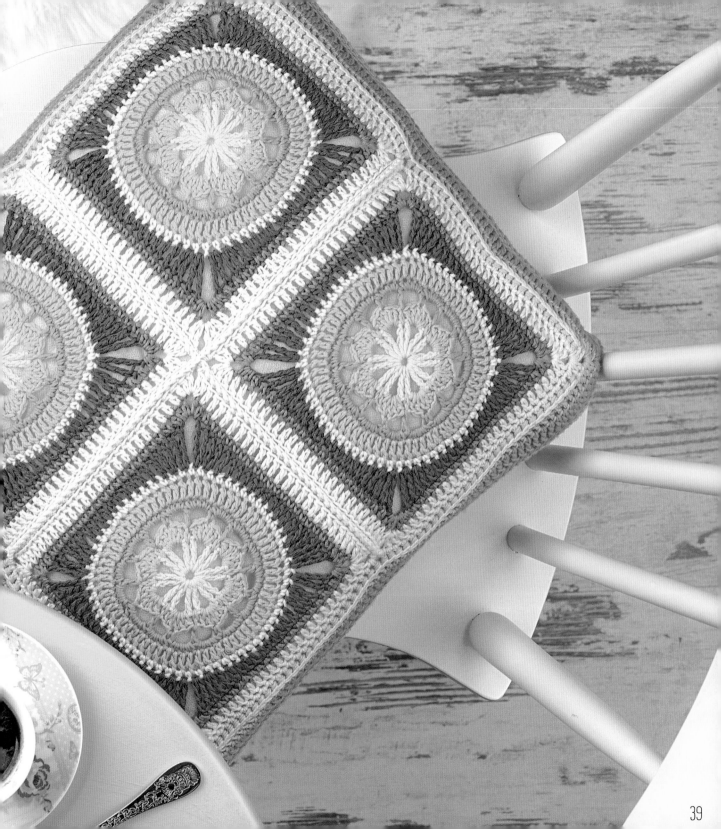

FINISHED SIZE

To fit 16″ (40.5 cm) Pillow Form
Each Motif – About 6 ¾″ (17 cm) square
Each 4-Motif Block (excluding Border) – About 13 ¼″ (34 cm)

MATERIALS

DMC Natura Just Cotton

> Color A – Ble (#83)
> Color B – Tournesol (#16)
> Color C – Giroflee (#85) 2 balls
> Color D – Nacar (#35)
> Color E – Blue Jeans (#26)
> Color F – Azur (#56)
> Color G – Ivory (#02)

One ball of each color was used, except for Color C.

Hook: Size E-4 (3.50 mm)

Scissors & Yarn Needle

16″ (40.5 cm) square Pillow Form

PATTERN NOTES

1 A Magic Ring (see Techniques) can be used instead of the chain ring in Round 1.
2 All joins are slip stitches, unless otherwise indicated.
3 All new colors are joined with right side facing, unless otherwise indicated.
4 Weave in all ends as you go.
5 Standing stitches (see Techniques) can be used to start a round with a new color.
6 An invisible join (see Techniques) can be used at the end of a round to finish a color.

SPECIAL STITCHES

Join With Single Crochet (join with sc): With slip knot on hook, insert hook into stitch or space indicated and pull up a loop (2 loops on hook). Yarn over and pull through both loops on hook (first single crochet made).

Double Treble (dtr): Yarn over hook three times, insert hook in stitch or space indicated and draw up a loop (five loops on hook). [Yarn over and pull yarn through two loops on hook] 4 times, until only one loop remains on hook.

Back Post Treble Crochet (BPtr): Yarn over hook twice, insert hook from back to front to back around post of indicated stitch, yarn over and draw up loop, [yarn over and pull through 2 loops] three times (treble crochet made).

CUSHION COVER

Motif (Make 8)

ROUND 1: *(Right Side)* Using Color A, ch 5, join with sl st to first ch to form ring; ch 4 (counts as first tr, now and throughout), tr in ring, ch 2, [2 tr in ring, ch 2] 7 times; join to first tr *(4ᵗʰ ch of beg ch-4)*. (16 tr & 8 ch-2 sps) Fasten off Color A.

ROUND 2: Using Color B, **join with sc** *(see Special Stitches)* to sp between any 2 adjacent tr-sts, [skip next tr, 5 dc in next ch-2 sp, skip next tr, sc in sp between tr-sts] around, omitting last sc on final repeat; join to first sc. (8 sc & 8 shells) Fasten off Color B.

ROUND 3: Join Color C with sl st to any sc, ch 5 *(counts as first dc & ch 2)*, [skip next 2 dc, sc in next (center) dc, ch 2, skip next 2 dc, dc in next sc] around, omitting last dc on final repeat; join to first dc *(3ʳᵈ ch of beg ch-5)*. (8 dc, 8 sc & 16 ch-2 sps)

ROUND 4: Ch 1, [4 sc in next ch-2 sp] around; join to first sc. (64 sc) Fasten off Color C.

ROUND 5: Join Color B with sl st to first sc, ch 3 (counts as first dc, now and throughout), [dc in next sc] around; join to first dc (3ʳᵈ ch of beg ch-3). (64 dc) Fasten off Color B.

ROUND 6: Using Color D, join with sc to first dc, [sc in next dc] around; join to first sc. (64 sc) Fasten off Color D.

ROUND 7: Join Color E with sl st to first dc, ch 5 *(counts as first dtr)*, dtr *(see Special Stitches)* in same st, *2 tr in next sc, tr in next sc, dc in each of next 4 sc, hdc in each of next 2 sc, dc in each of next 4 sc, tr in next sc, 2 tr in next sc, 2 dtr in next sc, ch 2**, 2 dtr in next sc; rep from * around, ending at ** on final repeat; join to first dtr *(5ᵗʰ ch of beg ch-5)*. (20 sts between each ch-2 corner – 4 dtr, 6 tr, 8 dc, 2 hdc) Fasten off Color E.

ROUND 8: Join Color F with sl st to any corner ch-2 sp, ch 2, (2 hdc, ch 2, 2 hdc) in same sp, *hdc in next dtr, sc in each of next 18 sts, hdc in next dtr**, (2 hdc, ch 2, 2 hdc) in next corner ch-2 sp; rep from * around, ending at ** on final repeat; join to first hdc. (24 sts between each ch-2 corner – 6 hdc & 18 sc) Fasten off Color F.

ROUND 9: Join Color G with sl st to any corner ch-2 sp, ch 3, (dc, ch 2, 2 dc) in same sp, dc in each of next 24 sts, [(2 dc, ch 2, 2 dc) in next ch-2 sp, dc in each of next 24 sts] around; join to first dc (3rd ch of beg ch-3) (112 dc & 4 ch-2 sps – 28 dc between corners) Fasten off Color G.

ASSEMBLY OF MOTIFS – Use photo as guide

Horizontal Seam
Holding 2 motifs with right sides facing (wrong sides together), matching shaping and stitches, working through both thicknesses, using Color G, join with sc to corner sp, sc in same sp, working in **back loops** of stitches only on both motifs, *sc in each of next 28 dc, 2 sc in corner ch-2 sp*, pick up next 2 motifs and work 2 sc in corner sp; rep from * to * once. (4 motifs joined across 2 sides) Fasten off Color G.

Vertical Seam
Using same 4 motifs, repeat Horizontal Seam to create a block of 4 motifs – 2 motifs wide by 2 motifs long.

Repeat Horizontal and Vertical Seams on remaining 4 Motifs, ending up with 2 blocks of 4 motifs each.

BLOCK BORDER
ROUND 1: With right side of one Block facing, join Color A with sl st to any outer corner ch-2 sp, ch 2, (2 hdc, ch 2, 2 hdc) in same sp, *hdc in each of next 28 dc, hdc in each of next 2 ch-2 sps (at seam), hdc in each of next 28 dc**, (2 hdc, ch 2, 2 hdc) in next corner ch-2 sp; join to first hdc; rep from * around, ending at ** on final repeat; join to first hdc. (248 hdc & 4 ch-2 corners – 62 hdc between corners) Fasten off Color A.

ROUND 2: Join Color B with sl st to any corner ch-2 sp, (2 hdc, ch 2, 2 hdc) in same sp, *hdc in each of next 2 hdc, **BPtr** (see Special Stitches) in each of next 58

hdc, hdc in each of next 2 hdc**, (2 hdc, ch 2, 2 hdc) in next corner ch-2 sp; rep from * around, ending at ** on final repeat. (32 hdc, 232 tr & 4 corner ch-2 sps – 66 sts between corners) Fasten off Color B.

ROUND 3: Join Color C with sl st to any corner ch-2 sp, ch 4, (tr, ch 2, 2 tr) in same sp, tr in each of next 66 sts, [(2 tr, ch 2, 2 tr) in next corner ch-2 sp, tr in each of next 66 sts] around; join to first tr (4th ch of beg ch-4). (280 tr & 4 corner ch-2 sps – 70 tr between corners) Fasten off Color C.

Repeat Block Border on second Block of Motifs.

ASSEMBLY OF CUSHION COVER – Use photo as guide

Holding the two complete Blocks with right sides facing (wrong sides together), matching shaping and stitches, working through both thicknesses, using Color C, join with sc to any corner ch-2 sp, 3 sc in same sp, working in **back loops** of stitches only on both blocks, *sc in each of next 70 tr, 4 sc in next corner ch-2 sp; rep from * twice more, insert Pillow form, sc in each of remaining 70 tr; join to first sc. (296 sc – 74 sc across each side) Fasten off Color C.

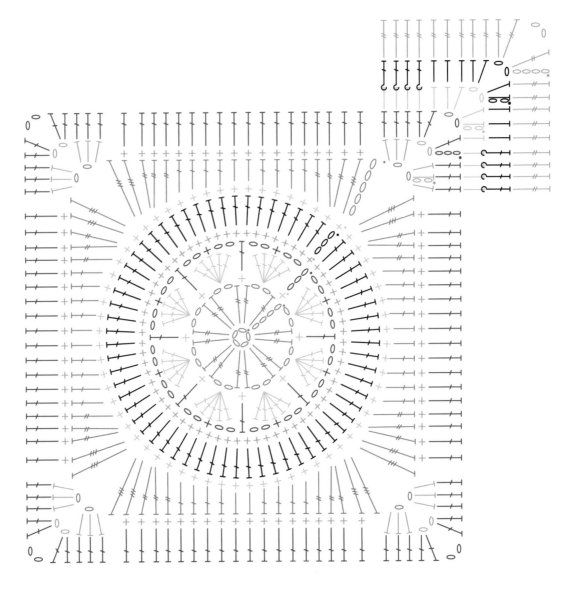

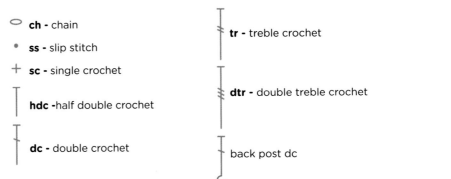

⬯	**ch -** chain
•	**ss -** slip stitch
+	**sc -** single crochet
(hdc symbol)	**hdc -** half double crochet
(dc symbol)	**dc -** double crochet
(tr symbol)	**tr -** treble crochet
(dtr symbol)	**dtr -** double treble crochet
(back post dc symbol)	back post dc

BLOOMING COASTERS

This is a lovely and simple pattern which works up quickly. The repetitive use of color adds a nice flow throughout the rounds. Are you feeling adventurous? Play around with various colors...

The only limit is your imagination. Looking for the perfect gift for someone? Why not make a set of coasters in the recipient's favorite colors.

Finished Size

For each Coaster - about 5 ¾" (14.5 cm) diameter

FINISHED SIZE

For each Coaster - about 5 ¾" (14.5 cm) diameter

MATERIALS

DMC Natura Just Cotton

    For 3-color Coasters
        Colors A, B & C – Azur (#56), Gardenia (#36) &
        Agatha (#44)
    For 5-color Coasters
        Colors A, B, C, D & E – Acanthe (#81),
        Lobelia (#82), Spring Rose (#07),
        Glacier (#87) & Turquoise (#49)

Hook: Size E-4 (3.50 mm)

Scissors & Yarn Needle

PATTERN NOTES

1 A Magic Ring *(see Techniques)* can be used instead of the chain ring in Round 1.
2 All joins are slip stitches, unless otherwise indicated.
3 All new colors are joined with right side facing, unless otherwise indicated.
4 Weave in all ends as you go.
5 Standing stitches *(see Techniques)* can be used to start a round with a new color.
6 An invisible join *(see Techniques)* can be used at the end of a round to finish a color.

SPECIAL STITCHES

Treble Cluster (tr-cl): Yarn over hook twice, insert hook in stitch or space indicated and draw up a loop (4 loops on hook), [yarn over, pull through 2 loops on hook] twice (2 loops on remain on hook), yarn over hook twice, insert hook in same stitch or space and draw up a loop, [yarn over, pull through 2 loops on hook] twice (3 loops remain on hook), yarn over, pull through all 3 loops on hook.

Join With Single Crochet (join with sc) - With slip knot on hook, insert hook into stitch or space indicated and pull up a loop (2 loops on hook). Yarn over and pull through both loops on hook (first single crochet made).

COASTER

Color Sequence of Rounds for 3-color Coasters: A, B, C, A, B, C, A, A
Color Sequence of Rounds for 5-color Coasters: A, B, C, D, E, A, B, C

ROUND 1: *(Right Side)* Starting with Color A, ch 4 join to first ch to form ring; ch 3 *(counts as first dc, now and throughout)*, 15 dc in ring; join to first dc *(3ʳᵈ ch of beg ch-3)*. (16 dc) Fasten off Color A.

ROUND 2: Join Color B with sl st to any dc, ch 4 *(counts as first dc & ch-1)*, [dc in next dc, ch 1] around; join to first dc *(3ʳᵈ ch of beg ch-3)*. (16 dc & 16 ch-1 sps) Fasten off Color B.

ROUND 3: Join Color C with sl st to any ch-1 sp, ch 3, tr in same sp *(first tr-cl made)*, ch 3, **tr-cl** *(see Special Stitches)* in next ch-1 sp, ch 3] around; join to first tr. (16 clusters & 16 ch-3 sps) Fasten off Color C.

ROUND 4: Join next color in sequence with sl st to any ch-3 sp, ch 2, 4 hdc in same sp, [4 hdc in next ch-3 sp] around; join to first hdc. (64 hdc) Fasten off.

ROUND 5: Using next color in sequence, join with sc to any hdc, [sc in next hdc] around; join to first sc. (64 sc) Fasten off.

ROUND 6: Join next color in sequence with sl st to any sc, ch 5 *(counts as first dc & ch-2)*, skip next sc, [dc in next sc, ch 2, skip next sc] around; join to first dc *(3ʳᵈ ch of beg ch-3)*. (32 dc & 32 ch-2 sps) Fasten off.

ROUND 7: Using next color in sequence, join with sc to any ch-2 sp, 2 sc in same sp, [3 sc in next ch-2 sp] around; join to first sc. (96 sc) Do NOT fasten off *(for 3-color Coaster)*. Fasten off *(for 5-color Coaster)*.

For 5-Color Coaster:

ROUND 8: Using next color, join with sc to first sc of any 3-sc group, [skip next 2 sc, 7 dc in next sc, skip next 2 sc, sc in next sc] around, omitting last sc on final repeat; join to first sc. (16 sc & 16 shells) Fasten off.

For 3-Color Coaster:

ROUND 8: Ch 1, sc in same st as joining, [skip next 2 sc, 7 dc in next sc, skip next 2 sc, sc in next sc] around, omitting last sc on final repeat; join to first sc. (16 sc & 16 shells) Fasten off.

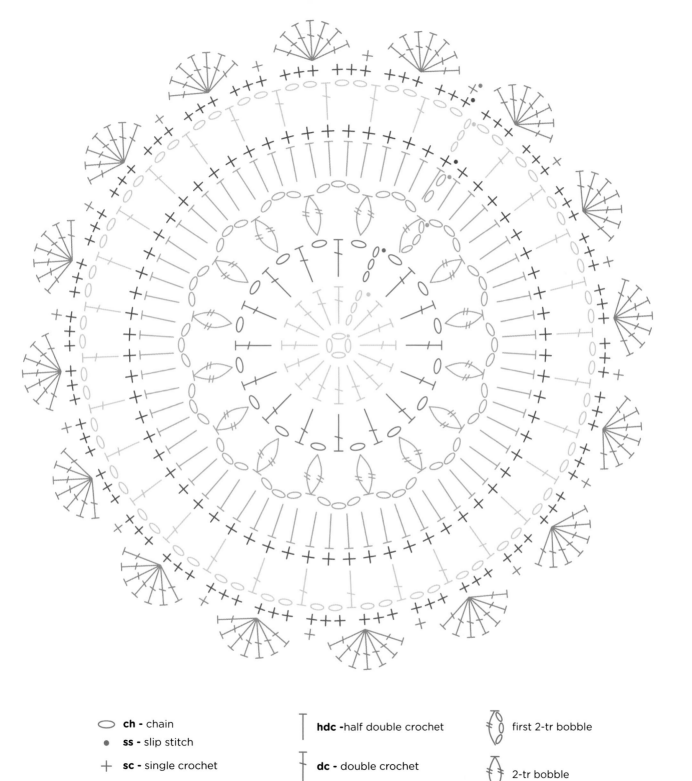

	ch - chain		**hdc -** half double crochet		first 2-tr bobble
	ss - slip stitch				
	sc - single crochet		**dc -** double crochet		2-tr bobble

BLOOMING PLACEMAT

The Blooming Placemat matches perfectly with the Blooming Coasters. I tried to keep the designs very similar for a more uniform look when they all placed nicely on the table. It was quite a learning curve making an oval-shaped design. There was a lot of 'frogging' but I am very happy with the end result.

Finished Size

About 12 ¼" (31 cm) wide,
10 ¼" (26 cm) deep

FINISHED SIZE

About 12 ¼" (31 cm) wide, 10 ¼" (26 cm) deep

MATERIALS

DMC Natura Just Cotton

> Color A – Acanthe (#81)
> Color B – Lobelia (#82)
> Color C – Spring Rose (#07)
> Color D – Glacier (#87)
> Color E – Turquoise (#49)

One ball of each color used to make one Placemat.

Hook: Size E-4 (3.50 mm)

Scissors & Yarn Needle

PATTERN NOTES

1 A Magic Ring (see Techniques) can be used instead of the chain ring in Round 1.
2 All joins are slip stitches, unless otherwise indicated.
3 All new colors are joined with right side facing, unless otherwise indicated.
4 Weave in all ends as you go.
5 Standing stitches (see Techniques) can be used to start a round with a new color.
6 An invisible join (see Techniques) can be used at the end of a round to finish a color.

SPECIAL STITCHES

Join With Single Crochet (join with sc): With slip knot on hook, insert hook into stitch or space indicated and pull up a loop (2 loops on hook). Yarn over and pull through both loops on hook (first single crochet made).

Beginning Treble Cluster (beg-tr-cl): Ch 3, yarn over hook twice, insert hook in stitch or space indicated and draw up a loop (3 loops on hook), [yarn over, pull through 2 loops on hook] twice.

Treble Cluster (tr-cl): Yarn over hook twice, insert hook in stitch or space indicated and draw up a loop (4 loops on hook), [yarn over, pull through 2 loops on hook] twice (2 loops on remain on hook), yarn over hook twice, insert hook in same stitch or space and draw up a loop, [yarn over, pull through 2 loops on hook] twice (3 loops remain on hook), yarn over, pull through all 3 loops on hook.

PLACEMAT

ROUND 1: *(Right Side)* Using Color A, ch 11, 3 hdc in 3rd ch from hook (skipped ch-sts do NOT count as first hdc), hdc in each of next 7 ch, 6 hdc in last ch, working in unused lps on other side of starting ch, hdc in each of next 7 ch, 3 hdc in last ch *(same ch as beg 3-hdc);* join to first hdc. (26 hdc)

ROUND 2: Ch 3 *(counts as first dc, now and throughout),* dc in same hdc as joining, 2 dc in each of next 2 hdc, dc in each of next 7 hdc, 2 dc in each of next 6 hdc, dc in each of next 7 hdc, 2 dc in each of next 3 hdc; join to first dc *(3rd ch of beg ch-3).* (38 dc)

ROUND 3: Ch 3, dc in same dc as joining, 2 dc in each of next 4 dc, dc in each of next 9 dc, 2 dc in each of next 10 dc, dc in each of next 9 dc, 2 dc in each of next 5 dc; join to first dc *(3rd ch of beg ch-3).* (58 dc)

ROUND 4: Ch 1, sc in same dc as joining, [ch 2, skip next dc, sc in next dc] around, omitting last sc on final repeat; join to first sc. (29 sc & 29 ch-2 sps) Fasten off Color A.

ROUND 5: Join Color B with sl st to first ch-2 sp, ch 4 (counts as first tr), 2 tr in same sp, [3 tr in next ch-2 sp] around; join to first tr *(4th ch of beg ch-4).* (87 tr) Fasten off Color B.

ROUND 6: Using Color C, **join with sc** *(see Special Stitches)* to first tr, [sc in next tr] around; join to first sc. (87 sc) Fasten off Color C.

ROUND 7: Join Color D with sl st to first sc, **beg-tr-cl** *(see Special Stitches)* in same st as joining, ch 4, skip next 2 sc, [**tr-cl** (see Special Stitches) in next sc, ch 4, skip next 2 sc] around; join to first tr. (29 clusters & 29 ch-4 lps) Fasten off Color D.

ROUND 8: Using Color E, join with sc to any ch-4 lp, 4 sc in same lp, [5 sc in next ch-4 lp] around; join to first sc. (145 sc) Fasten off Color E.

ROUND 9: Join Color A with sl st to first sc, ch 7 *(counts as first dc & ch-4),* skip next 4 sc, [(dc, ch 4, dc) in next sc, skip next 4 sc] around; join to first dc *(3rd ch of beg ch-7).* (58 dc & 29 ch-4 lps)

ROUND 10: Sl st in next ch-4 lp, ch 3, (2 dc, ch 1, 3 dc) in same lp, [(3 dc, ch 1, 3 dc) in next ch-4 lp around; join to first dc (*3rd ch of beg ch-3*). (174 dc & 29 ch-1 sps) Fasten off Color A.

ROUND 11: Join Color C with sl st to any ch-1 sp, ch 8 *(counts as first dc & ch-5)*, skip next 6 dc, [dc in next ch-1 sp, ch 5, skip next 6 dc] around; join to first dc (*3rd ch of beg ch-8*) (29 dc & 29 ch-5 lps) Fasten off Color C.

ROUND 12: Join Color D with sl st to any ch-5 lp, ch 3, 5 dc in same lp, [6 dc in next ch-5 lp] around; join to first dc (*3rd ch of beg ch-3*). (174 dc) Fasten off Color D.

ROUND 13: Using Color E, join with sc to first dc, [sc in next dc] around; join to first sc. (174 sc)

ROUND 14: Ch 1, sc in same st, [skip next 2 sc, 7 dc in next sc, skip next 2 sc, sc in next sc] around, omitting last sc on final repeat; join to first sc. (29 sc & 29 shells) Fasten off Color E.

⬯	**ch -** chain
•	**ss -** slip stitch
+	**sc -** single crochet
T	**hdc -**half double crochet
†	**dc -** double crochet
‡	**tr -** treble crochet
	first 2-tr bobble
	2-tr bobble

51

FLOWER PATCH CUSHION

I originally designed this crochet motif using a thinner yarn, but after looking at it, I decided I wanted something different… Not the usual patchwork-type cushion. So I went big… and chunky. You can see that I've used my favorite popcorn stitches again. Here they remind me of tulips and roses, hence the name of this design -
'Flower Patch'.

Finished Size

About 10" (25.5 cm) diameter

Hook: Size E-4 (3.50 mm)

FINISHED SIZE

About 18" (46 cm) square

MATERIALS

DMC Natura Just Cotton XL

Color A – Lagoon (#07)	1 ball
Color B – Aqua (#73)	2 balls
Color C – Ecru (#03)	2 balls
Color D (Front) – Rose (#04)	1 ball
Color D (Back) – Orange (#42)	1 ball

Hook: Size K-10 ½ (6.50 mm)

Scissors & Yarn Needle

18" square Cushion form

PATTERN NOTES

1 A Magic Ring *(see Techniques)* can be used instead of the chain ring in Round 1.
2 All joins are slip stitches, unless otherwise indicated.
3 All new colors are joined with right side facing, unless otherwise indicated.
4 Weave in all ends as you go.
5 Standing stitches *(see Techniques)* can be used to start a round with a new color.
6 An invisible join *(see Techniques)* can be used at the end of a round to finish a color.

SPECIAL STITCHES

Beginning Popcorn (beg-pc): Ch 3, 4 dc in same st or sp indicated, drop lp from hook, insert hook from front to back in first dc made *(3rd ch of beg ch-3)*, pull dropped lp through, ch 1 (to lock). First popcorn made.

Popcorn (pc): Work 5 dc in same stitch or space indicated, drop lp from hook, insert hook from front to back in first dc made, pull dropped lp through, ch 1 (to lock).

Join With Single Crochet (join with sc) - With slip knot on hook, insert hook into stitch or space indicated and pull up a loop (2 loops on hook). Yarn over and pull through both loops on hook (first single crochet made).

Back Post Single Crochet (BPsc): Insert hook from back to front to back around post of indicated stitch, yarn over and draw up loop, yarn over and pull through both loops on hook (single crochet made).

Treble Bobble (2-tr bobble): Yarn over hook twice, insert hook in stitch or space indicated and draw up a loop (4 loops on hook), [yarn over, pull through 2 loops on hook] twice (2 loops on remain on hook), yarn over hook twice, insert hook in same stitch or space and draw up a loop, [yarn over, pull through 2 loops on hook] twice (3 loops remain on hook), yarn over, pull through all 3 loops on hook.

CUSHION COVER

SIDES – Make 2

ROUND 1: *(Right Side)* Using Color A, ch 7; join with sl st to first ch to form a ring; ch 1, [sc in ring, ch 1] 8 times; join to first sc. (8 sc & 8 ch-1 sps)

ROUND 2: Sl st in next ch-1 sp, **beg-pc** *(see Special Stitches)*, ch 3, [**pc** *(see Special Stitches)* in next ch-1 sp, ch 3] around; join to top of first pc. (8 popcorns & 8 ch-3 sps) Fasten off Color A.

ROUND 3: Using Color B, **join with sc** *(see Special Stitches)* in any ch-3 sp, 4 sc in same sp, [5 sc in next ch-3 sp] around; join to first sc. (40 sc) Fasten off Color B.

Note: When working in the back loops, I suggest working through the back loop together with the loop below the back loop (third loop). This makes the stitch more stable and doesn't leave any holes.

ROUND 4: Using Color C, join with sc to **back loop** of first sc, working in **back loops** only, [sc in next sc] around; join to first sc. (40 sc) Fasten off Color C.

ROUND 5: Using Color A, join with sc to first sc, sc in next sc, *(sc, dc in front loop of corresponding sc on Rnd 3, sc) in next sc**, sc in each of next 4 sc; rep from * around, ending at ** on final repeat, sc in each of next 2 sc; join to first sc. (48 sc & 8 dc) Fasten off Color A.

ROUND 6: Join Color D with sl st to any dc, beg-pc, sc in each of next 6 sc, [pc in next dc, sc in each of next 6 sc] around; join to top of first pc. (8 popcorns & 48 sc) Fasten off Color D.

ROUND 7: Using Color B, join with sc to any pc, sc in each of next 2 sc, 2 sc in next sc, [sc in each of next 6 sts,

2 sc in next sc] around, ending sc in each of next 3 sc; join to first sc. (64 sc) Fasten off Color B.

ROUND 8: Using Color C, join with sc to **back loop** of first sc, working in **back loops** only, [sc in next sc] around; join to first sc. (64 sc) Fasten off Color C.

ROUND 9: Using Color A, sc in first sc, sc in each of next 4 sc, *dc in front loop on corresponding sc on Rnd 7**, sc in each of next 8 sc; rep from * around, ending at ** on final repeat, sc in each of next 3 sc; join to first sc. (64 sc & 8 dc) Fasten off Color A.

ROUND 10: Join Color D with sl st to any dc, beg-pc, sc in each of next 8 sc, [pc in next dc, sc in each of next 8 sc] around; join to top of first pc. (8 popcorns & 64 sc) Fasten off Color D.

ROUND 11: Using Color B, join with sc to any pc, [sc in next st] around; join to first sc. (72 sc) Fasten off Color B.

ROUND 12: Join Color D with sl st to first sc, ch 3, dc in same st as joining, dc in each of next 2 sc, [2 dc in next sc, dc in each of next 2 sc] around; join to first dc (*3rd ch of beg ch-3*). (96 dc) Fasten off Color D.

ROUND 13: Join Color A with sl st to 2nd dc, ch 3, tr in same st as joining (*first tr-cl made*), ch 2, (**tr-cl** (see Special Stitches), ch 2, 2-tr bobble) in same st, *ch 1, skip next 3 dc, hdc in each of next 3 dc, **BPsc** (*see Special Stitches*) in each of next 11 dc, hdc in each of next 3 dc, ch 1, skip next 3 dc**, (tr-cl, [ch2, tr-cl] twice) in next dc; rep from * around, ending at ** on final repeat; join to first tr. (12 tr-cl (4 groups), 24 hdc, 44 sc & 8 ch-1 sps) Fasten off Color A.

ROUND 14: Using Color B, join with sc to center tr-cl of any 3-tr-cl group, ch 1, sc in same st, *2 sc in next ch-2 sp, sc in next tr-cl, sc in next ch-1 sp, sc in each of next 17 sts, sc in next ch-1 sp, sc in next tr-cl, 2 sc in next ch-2 sp**, (sc, ch 1, sc) in next tr-cl; rep from * around, ending at ** on final repeat; join to first sc. (108 sc & 4 corner ch-1 sps) Fasten off Color B.

ROUND 15: Join Color C with sl st to any corner ch-1 sp, ch 5 (*counts as first dc & ch-2, now and throughout*), dc in same sp, *dc in each of next 27 sc**, (dc, ch 2, dc) in next corner ch-1 sp; rep from * around, ending at ** on final repeat; join to first dc (*3rd ch of beg ch-5*). (116 dc & 4 corner ch-2 sps)

ROUND 16: Sl st in next ch-2 sp, ch 5, dc in same sp, *dc in each of next 29 dc**, (dc, ch 2, dc) in next corner ch-2 sp; rep from * around, ending at ** on final repeat; join to first dc (*3rd ch of beg ch-5*). (124 dc & 4 corner ch-2 sps) Fasten off Color C.

CUSHION ASSEMBLY – Use photo as guide

Holding both Sides with right sides facing (wrong sides together), matching stitches and working through both thicknesses, using Color B, join with sc to any corner ch-2 sp, (sc, ch 1, 2 sc) in same sp, *working in the **back loops** only on both Sides, sc in each of next 31 dc**, (2 sc, ch 1, 2 sc) in next corner ch-2 sp; rep from * twice more, insert cushion form, rep from * to ** once; join to first sc. Fasten off Color B.

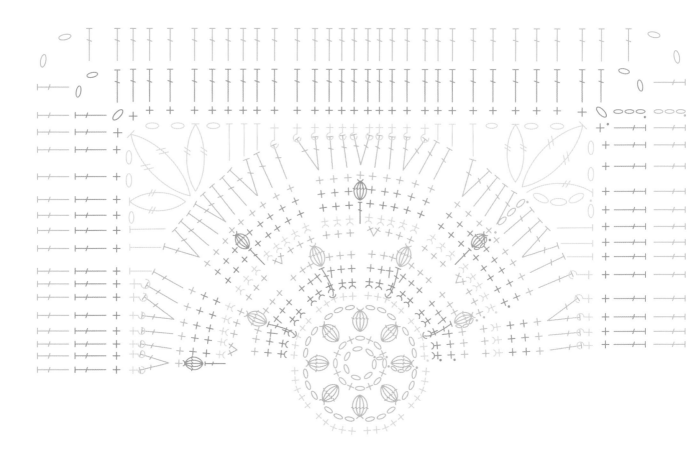

 ch - chain

ss - slip stitch

sc - single crochet

single crochet in back loop

back post single crochet

hdc - half double crochet

dc - double crochet

 2-tr bobble

 beginning 2-tr bobble

 5-dc popcorn

 beginning popcorn

DANCING AROUND IN CIRCLES

This was the first design I made for my book. It was a dream of mine to become an author. Something I never thought would happen. So naturally, as soon as I found out it would become a reality, I picked up my hook and yarn and started 'croodling' (crochet-doodling), not knowing what would come on the next round… Impromptu crochet?

This simple design is worked in ten rounds, and my favorite colors in this piece are the yellow and warmer tones as it reminds me of figures dancing around in circles.

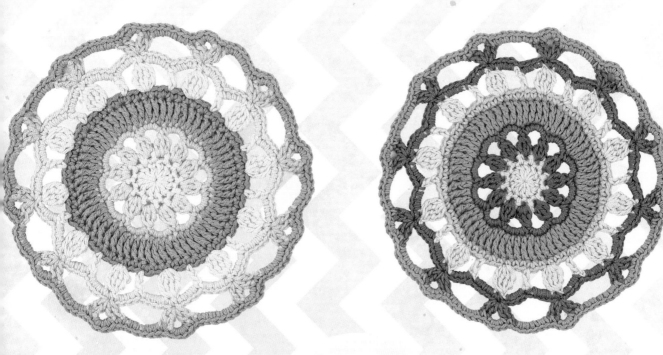

Finished Size

About 7" (18 cm) diameter

FINISHED SIZE

About 7" (18 cm) diameter

MATERIALS

DMC Natura Just Cotton

Color A - Ble (#83)

Color B - Acanthe (#81)

Color C - Lobelia (#82)

Color D - Sping Rose (#07)

Color E - Cerise (#62)

One ball of each color was used for the pictured Doily.

Hook: Size E-4 (3.50 mm)

Scissors & Yarn Needle

PATTERN NOTES

1 A Magic Ring *(see Techniques)* can be used instead of the chain ring in Round 1.

2 All joins are slip stitches, unless otherwise indicated.

3 All new colors are joined with right side facing, unless otherwise indicated.

4 Weave in all ends as you go.

5 Standing stitches *(see Techniques)* can be used to start a round with a new color.

6 An invisible join *(see Techniques)* can be used at the end of a round to finish a color.

SPECIAL STITCHES

Beginning Cluster (beg-cl): Ch 2, *yarn over, insert hook in same stitch or space and draw up a loop, yarn over, pull through 2 loops on hook; repeat from * once more (3 loops remain on hook), yarn over, pull through all 3 loops on hook (first Cluster made).

Cluster (cl): Yarn over, insert hook in stitch or space indicated and draw up a loop (3 loops on hook), yarn over, pull through 2 loops on hook (2 loops on remain on hook), *yarn over, insert hook in same stitch or space and draw up a loop, yarn over, pull through 2 loops on hook; repeat from * once more (4 loops remain on hook), yarn over, pull through all 4 loops on hook.

Treble Bobble (tr-bob): Yarn over hook twice, insert hook in stitch or space indicated and draw up a loop (4 loops on hook), [yarn over, pull through 2 loops on hook] twice (2 loops on remain on hook), *yarn over hook twice, insert hook in same stitch or space and draw up a loop, [yarn over, pull through 2 loops on hook] twice; repeat from * twice more (5 loops remain on hook), yarn over, pull through all 5 loops on hook.

Join With Single Crochet (join with sc) - With slip knot on hook, insert hook into stitch or space indicated and pull up a loop (2 loops on hook). Yarn over and pull through both loops on hook (first single crochet made).

DOILY

ROUND 1: *(Right Side)* Starting with Color A, ch 4; join to first ch to form ring; ch 3 (counts as first dc, now and throughout), 11 dc in ring; join to first dc (3rd ch of beg ch-3). (12 dc)

ROUND 2: [Ch 3, sl st in next dc] 12 times. (12 ch-3 lps) Fasten off Color A.

ROUND 3: Join Color B to any ch-3 lp, beg-cl *(see Special Stitches)* in same lp, ch 4, [cl *(see Special Stitches)* in next ch-3 lp, ch 4] around; join to top of first cluster. (12 clusters & 12 ch-4 lps) Fasten off Color B.

ROUND 4: Join Color C to top of any cluster, ch 1, [5 sc in next ch-4 lp] around; join to first sc. (60 sc) Fasten off Color C.

ROUND 5: Join Color D to any sc, ch 4 *(counts as first tr, now and throughout)*, [tr in next sc] around; join to first tr *(4th ch of beg ch-4)*. (60 tr) Fasten off Color D.

ROUND 6: Using Color E, join with sc (see Special Stitches) to any tr, sc in same st as joining, sc in each of next 4 tr, [2 sc in next tr, sc in each of next 4 tr] around; join to first sc. (72 sc) Fasten off Color E.

ROUND 7: Join Color A to any sc, ch 7 *(counts as first dc & ch-4)*, skip next 2 sc, tr-bob *(see Special Stitches)* in next sc, ch 4, skip next 2 sc, [dc in next sc, ch 4, skip next 2 sc, tr-bob in next sc, ch 4, skip next 2 sc] around; join to first dc *(3rd ch of beg ch-7)*. (12 bobbles, 12 dc & 24 ch-4 lps) Fasten off Color A.

ROUND 8: Join Color B to any dc-st, ch 1, [4 sc in next ch-4 sp, 2 sc in top of next bobble, 4 sc in next ch-4 sp, skip next dc] around; join to first sc. (120 sc) Fasten off Color B.

ROUND 9: Join Color C to 2nd sc on any bob, ch 3, (dc, ch 3, 2 dc) in same st as joining, ch 6, skip next 9 sc, [(2 dc, ch 3, 2 dc) in next sc, ch 6, skip next 9 sc] around; join to first dc *(3rd ch of beg ch-3)*. (12 shells & 12 ch-6 lps) Fasten off Color C.

ROUND 10: Using Color D, join with sc to first dc of any shell, skip next dc, 4 sc in next ch-3 sp, skip next dc, sc in next dc, 6 sc in next ch-6 lp, [sc in next dc, skip next dc, 4 sc in next ch-3 sp, skip next dc, sc in next dc, 6 sc in next ch-6 lp] around; join to first sc. (144 sc) Fasten off Color D.

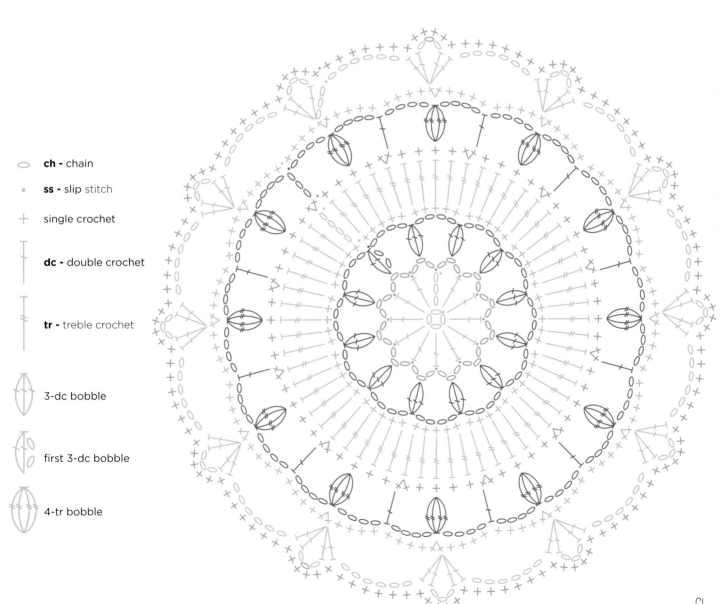

⬯	**ch** - chain
•	**ss** - slip stitch
+	single crochet
┬	**dc** - double crochet
╪	**tr** - treble crochet
⬯	3-dc bobble
⬯	first 3-dc bobble
⬯	4-tr bobble

SWEET SUNSHINE DOILY

I was wanting something a little more dimensional and eye-catching with this design. There was a fair bit of frogging (undoing what had just be done) in this piece, as I either didn't like the look of it, nor was it going to work the way I had imagined. Nevertheless, I am more than happy with the final result.

The use of back post stitches really makes the previous rounds 'pop'. I love the final edging on this piece as it reminds me of flares of the sun.

Finished Size

About 10" (25.5 cm) diameter

FINISHED SIZE
About 10" (25.5 cm) diameter

MATERIALS

DMC Natura Just Cotton
Color A - Ble (#83)
Color B - Cerise (#62)
Color C - Blue Jeans (#26)
Color D - Bleu Layette (#05)
Color E - Aquamarina (#25)

One ball of each color was used for the pictured Doily.

Hook: Size E-4 (3.50 mm)

Scissors & Yarn Needle

PATTERN NOTES

1 A Magic Ring *(see Techniques)* can be used instead of the chain ring in Round 1.
2 All joins are slip stitches, unless otherwise indicated.
3 All new colors are joined with right side facing, unless otherwise indicated.
4 Weave in all ends as you go.
5 Standing stitches *(see Techniques)* can be used to start a round with a new color.
6 An invisible join *(see Techniques)* can be used at the end of a round to finish a color.
7 Blocking the finished doily is recommended to keep the picots looking lovely.

SPECIAL STITCHES

Join With Single Crochet (join with sc) - With slip knot on hook, insert hook into stitch or space indicated and pull up a loop (2 loops on hook). Yarn over and pull through both loops on hook (first single crochet made).

Back Post Treble Crochet (BPtr): Yarn over hook twice, insert hook from back to front to back around post of indicated stitch, yarn over and draw up loop, [yarn over and pull through 2 loops] three times (treble crochet made).

Back Post Double Crochet (BPdc): Yarn over hook, insert hook from back to front to back around post of indicated stitch, yarn over and draw up loop, [yarn over and pull through 2 loops] twice (double crochet made).

Three-Chain Picot (p3): Chain 3, insert hook back into the center of the base stitch (through both the front loop and loop below the front loop), yarn over and pull through stitch and loops on hook (slip stitch made).

Five-Chain Picot (p5): Chain 5, insert hook back into the center of the base stitch (through both the front loop and loop below the front loop), yarn over and pull through stitch and loops on hook (slip stitch made).

Seven-Chain Picot (p7): Chain 7, insert hook back into the center of the base stitch (through both the front loop and loop below the front loop), yarn over and pull through stitch and loops on hook (slip stitch made).

DOILY

ROUND 1: *(Right Side)* Starting with Color A, ch 4; join to first ch to form ring; ch 3 (counts as first dc, now and throughout), 11 dc in ring; join to first dc *(3rd ch of beg ch-3)*. (12 dc)

ROUND 2: Ch 3, dc in same st as joining, [2 dc in next dc] around; join to first dc. (24 dc) Fasten off Color A.

ROUND 3: Using Color B, join with sc *(see Special Stitches)* to any dc, 2 sc in next dc, [sc in next dc, 2 sc in next dc] around; join to first sc. (36 sc)

ROUND 4: Ch 2, dc in same st as joining, (dc, ch 2, sl st) in next sc, [(sl st, ch 2, dc) in next sc, (dc, ch 2, sl st) in next sc] around; join to top of beg ch-2. (36 dc & 36 ch-2 sts) Fasten off Color B.

ROUND 5: Join Color C to sp between any 2 adjacent dc-sts (not ch-2 sts), ch 3, skip next 4 sts *(dc, 2 x ch-2, dc)*, [sl st in sp between next dc-sts, ch 3, skip next 4 sts] around; join to first ch-3 lp. (18 ch-3 lps)

ROUND 6: Ch 1, 4 sc in same lp, [4 sc in next ch-3 lp] around; join to first sc. (72 sc) Fasten off Color C.

ROUND 7: Join Color D to any sc, ch 3, [dc in next sc] around; join to first dc *(3rd ch of beg ch-3)*. (72 dc) Fasten off Color D.

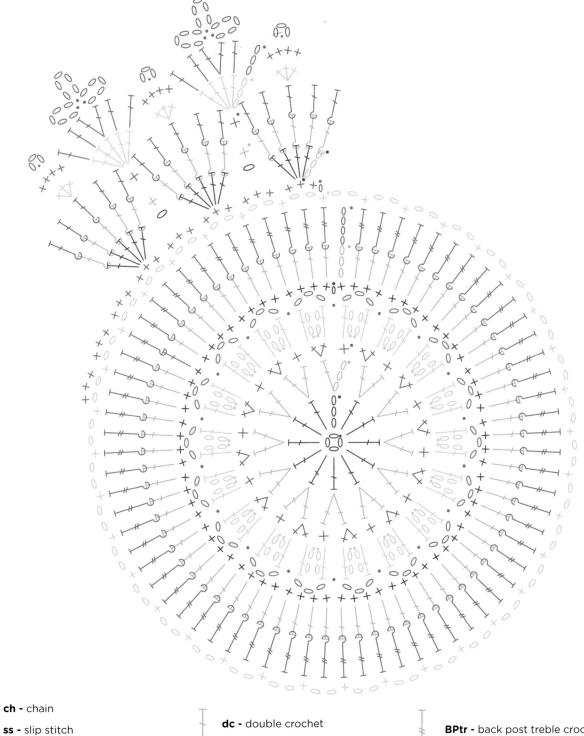

⬭ **ch -** chain	ꟾ **dc -** double crochet
• **ss -** slip stitch	
+ **sc -** single crochet	ꟾ **BPdc -** back post double crochet
0̤0 picot	ꟾ **BPtr -** back post treble crochet

ROUND 8: Join Color E around back post of any dc, ch 4 *(counts as first tr)*, [BPtr *(see Special Stitches)* in next dc] around; join to first tr *(4th ch of beg ch-4)*. (72 tr) Fasten off Color E.

ROUND 9: Using Color A, join with sc to any tr, ch 2, skip next tr, [sc in next tr, ch 2, skip next tr] around; join to first sc. (36 sc & 36 ch-2 lps)

ROUND 10: Ch 1, [3 sc in next ch-2 lp] around; join to first sc. (108 sc)

ROUND 11: Sl st in next *(center)* sc, ch 3, 4 dc in same sc, ch 1, skip next 5 sc, [5 dc in next *(center)* sc, ch 1, skip next 5 sc] around; join to first dc *(3rd ch of beg ch-3)*. (18 shells & 18 ch-1 sps) Fasten off Color A.

ROUND 12: Using Color B, join with sc to any ch-1 sp, BPdc *(see Special Stitches)* in each of next 5 dc, [sc in next ch-1 sp, BPdc in each of next 5 dc] around; join to first sc. (18 groups of 5-dc & 18 sc) Fasten off Color B.

ROUND 13: Using Color C, join with sc to any sc, [BPdc in each of next 5 dc, sc in next sc] around, omitting last sc on final repeat; join to first sc. (18 groups of 5-dc & 18 sc) Fasten off Color C.

ROUND 14: Join Color D to any sc, ch 3, 4 dc in same sc, skip next 2 dc, 3 sc in next *(center)* dc, skip next 2 dc, [5 dc in next sc, skip next 2 dc, 3 sc in next *(center)* dc, skip next 2 dc] around; join to first dc *(3rd ch of beg ch-3)*. (18 groups of 5-dc & 18 groups of 3-sc) Fasten off Color D.

ROUND 15: Join Color E to first dc of any 5-dc group, ch 3, dc in next dc, (dc, p5 *(see Special Stitches)*), p7 *(see Special Stitches)*, p5, dc) in next *(center)* dc, dc in each of next 2 dc, sc in next sc, (sc, p3 *(see Special Stitches)*, sc) in next *(center)* sc, sc in next sc, *dc in each of next 2 dc, (dc, p5, p7, p5, dc) in next *(center)* dc, dc in each of next 2 dc, sc in next sc, (sc, p3, sc) in next *(center)* sc, sc in next sc; rep from * around; join to first dc *(3rd ch of beg ch-3)*. (108 dc, 72 sc, 18 small picots & 18 large picot groups) Fasten off Color E.

PRIMROSE PATCH RUG

I had an absolute blast designing and crocheting this piece. The chunky yarn works up so quickly, and its soft feel is lovely. I will admit I have a soft spot for popcorn stitches. This design could be made in a finer yarn, resulting in a smaller doily. The soft pastel colors of aqua and grey bring a calming effect to any room this rug is placed in. Why not play with colors to suit your décor?

Finished Size

About 35" (89 cm) diameter

FINISHED SIZE

About 35″ (89 cm) diameter

MATERIALS

DMC Natura Just Cotton XL

    Color A – Cloud (#12)   3 balls
    Color B – Aqua (#73)   2 balls

Hook: Size K-10½ (6.50 mm)

Scissors & Yarn Needle

PATTERN NOTES

1 A Magic Ring *(see Techniques)* can be used instead of the chain ring in Round 1.
2 All joins are slip stitches, unless otherwise indicated.
3 All new colors are joined with right side facing, unless otherwise indicated.
4 Weave in all ends as you go.
5 Standing stitches *(see Techniques)* can be used to start a round with a new color.
6 An invisible join *(see Techniques)* can be used at the end of a round to finish a color.

SPECIAL STITCHES

Beginning Cluster (beg-cl): Ch 2, *yarn over, insert hook in same stitch or space and draw up a loop, yarn over, pull through 2 loops on hook; repeat from * once more (3 loops remain on hook), yarn over, pull through all 3 loops on hook (first Cluster made).

Cluster (cl): Yarn over, insert hook in stitch or space indicated and draw up a loop (3 loops on hook), yarn over, pull through 2 loops on hook (2 loops on remain on hook), *yarn over, insert hook in same stitch or space and draw up a loop, yarn over, pull through 2 loops on hook; repeat from * once more (4 loops remain on hook), yarn over, pull through all 4 loops on hook.

Join With Single Crochet (join with sc) - With slip knot on hook, insert hook into stitch or space indicated and pull up a loop (2 loops on hook). Yarn over and pull through both loops on hook (first single crochet made).

Popcorn (pc): Work 5 dc in same stitch or space indicated, drop lp from hook, insert hook from front to back in first dc made, pull dropped lp through.

V-Stitch (v-st): Work (dc, ch 3, dc) in same stitch or space indicated.

RUG

ROUND 1: *(Right Side)* Starting with Color A, ch 5; join to first ch to form ring; ch 3 (counts as first dc, now and throughout), 15 dc in ring; join to first dc *(3rd ch of beg ch-3)*. (16 dc)

ROUND 2: Ch 6 *(counts as first tr & ch-2, now and throughout)*, [tr in next dc, ch 2] around; join to first tr *(4th ch of beg ch-6)*. (16 tr & 16 ch-2 sps)

ROUND 3: Sl st in next ch-2 sp, **beg-cl** *(see Special Stitches)* in same sp, ch 4, [**cl** *(see Special Stitches)* in next ch-2 sp, ch 4] around; join to top of first cl. (16 clusters & 16 ch-4 lps)

ROUND 4: Sl st in each of next 2 ch, sl st in ch-4 lp, ch 5, [sl st in next ch-4 lp, ch 5] around; sl st in first ch-5 lp. (16 ch-5 lps)

ROUND 5: Ch 1, (3 sc, ch 1, 3 sc) in same lp, [(3 sc, ch 1, 3 sc) in next ch-5 lp] around; join to first sc. (96 sc & 16 ch-1 sps) Fasten off Color A.

ROUND 6: Using Color B, **join with sc** *(see Special Stitches)* to any ch-1 sp, ch 4, [sc in next ch-1 sp, ch 4] around; join to first sc. (16 sc & 16 ch-4 lps)

ROUND 7: Sl st in next ch-4 sp, ch 3 (counts as first dc, now and throughout), 5 dc in same sp, [6 dc in next ch-4 sp] around; join to first dc *(3rd ch of beg ch-3)*. (96 dc)

ROUND 8: Ch 2 *(does NOT count as first st)*, hdc in same st as joining, [hdc in next dc] around; join to first hdc. (96 hdc)

ROUND 9: Ch 6, skip next hdc, [tr in next hdc, ch 2, skip next hdc] around; join to first tr (*4th ch of beg ch-6*). (48 tr & 48 ch-2 sps)

ROUND 10: Sl st in next ch-2 sp, beg-cl in same sp, ch 3, [cl in next ch-2 sp, ch 3] around; join to top of first cl. (48 clusters & 48 ch-3 lps)

ROUND 11: Ch 1, [3 sc in each ch-3 lp] around; join to first sc. (144 sc)

ROUND 12: Ch 1, sc in same st as joining, **pc** (*see Special Stitches*) in next (*center*) sc, sc in each of next 2 sc, 3 sc in next (*center*) sc, sc in each of next 2 sc, *pc in next (*center*) sc, sc in each of next 2 sc, 3 sc in next (*center*) sc, sc in each of next 2 sc; rep from * around, omitting last sc on final repeat; join to first sc. (24 popcorns & 168 sc) Fasten off Color B.

ROUND 13: Join Color A to center sc of any 3-sc group, ch 6 (*counts as first dc & ch-3*), dc in same st as joining (*first v-st made*), *ch 2, skip next 3 sc, dc in next pc, ch 2, skip next 3 sc, v-st (see Special Stitches) in next (*center*) sc; rep from * around, omitting last **v-st** on final repeat; join to first dc (*3rd ch of beg ch-6*). (24 v-sts, 24 dc & 48 ch-2 sps)

ROUND 14: Sl st in next ch-3 sp (*of v-st*), ch 3, 4 dc in same sp, ch 2, skip next ch-2 sp, sc in next dc, ch 2, skip next ch-2 sp, [5 dc in next v-st, ch 2, sc in next dc, ch 2] around; join to first dc (*3rd ch of beg ch-3*). (120 dc, 24 sc & 48 ch-2 sps)

ROUND 15: Ch 4 (*counts as first dc & ch-1*), [dc in next dc, ch 1] 4 times, skip next ch-2 sp, sc in next sc, ch 1, skip next ch-2 sp, *[dc in next dc, ch 1] 5 times, sc in next sc, ch 1; rep from * around; join to first dc (*3rd ch of beg ch-4*). (120 dc, 24 sc & 144 ch-1 sps)

ROUND 16: [Sl st in next ch-1 sp, sl st in next dc] twice, ch 1, sc in same (*center*) dc, [ch 8, skip next 11 sts, sc in next (*center*) dc] around, omitting last sc on final repeat; join to first sc. (24 sc & 24 ch-8 lps)

ROUND 17: Ch 1, [10 sc in next ch-8 lp] around; join to first sc. (*240 sc*)

ROUND 18: Ch 3, [dc in next sc] around; join to first dc (*3rd ch of beg ch-3*). (240 dc)

ROUND 19: Ch 1, sc in same st as joining, sc in each of next 5 dc, *ch 1, skip next 3 dc, (dc, ch 3, tr) in next dc, (tr, ch 3, tr) in next dc, (tr, ch 3, dc) in next dc, ch 1, skip next 3 dc, sc in each of next 11 dc; rep from * around, ending ch 1, skip next 3 dc, (dc, ch 3, tr) in next dc, (tr, ch 3, tr) in next dc, (tr, ch 3, dc) in next dc, ch 1, skip next 3 dc, sc in each of next 5 dc; join to first sc. (24 dc, 48 tr, 132 sc, 24 ch-1 sps & 36 ch-3 sps) Fasten off Color A.

ROUND 20: Join Color B to same sc as Rnd 19 joining, ch 5 (*counts as first tr & ch-1*), ([tr, ch 1] twice) in same sc, *skip next 2 sc, sc in next sc, ch 1, sc in next sc, skip next sc, [5 dc in next ch-3 sp, sl st in sp between tr-sts] twice, 5 dc in next ch-3 sp, skip next sc, [sc in next sc, ch 1] twice, skip next 2 sc**, ([tr, ch 1] 3 times) in next (*center*) sc; rep from * around, ending at ** on final repeat; join to first tr (*4th ch of beg ch-5*). (36 tr, 180 dc, 48 sc, 24 sl sts & 72 ch-1 sps) Fasten off Color B.

ch - chain

ss - slip stitch

sc - single crochet

hdc - half double crochet

dc - double crochet

tr - treble crochet

first 3-dc bobble

3-dc bobble

5-dc popcorn

STARS IN THE NIGHT SKY

I wanted to make a piece where motifs were joined together "as-you-go". So, say 'hello' to this striking centerpiece, Stars in the Night Sky. I used the white as a contrasting color to make the stars stand out. This design could be made larger by making and joining more motifs until you reach the size desired. Perhaps you'd like to make a blanket, throw or even a shawl. If you are feeling adventurous, use DMC Chunky and turn this stunner into a fabulous rug.

Finished Size

About 16" (40.5 cm) across
(widest point)

FINISHED SIZE
About 16" (40.5 cm) across (widest point)

MATERIALS

DMC Natura Just Cotton
Main Color - Ibiza (#01)
  Center Motif 1:
    Color A - Tournesol (#16)
    Color B - Giroflee (#85)
  Motifs 2 & 5:
    Color A - Glacier (#87)
    Color B - Aguamarine (#25)
  Motifs 3 & 6:
    Color A - Bleu Layette (#05)
    Color B - Blue Jeans (#26)
  Motifs 4 & 7:
    Color A - Spring Rose (#07)
    Color B - Cerise (#62)
One ball of each color was used for the pictured Centerpiece.

Hook: Size E-4 (3.50 mm)

Scissors & Yarn Needle

PATTERN NOTES

1 A Magic Ring *(see Techniques)* can be used instead of the chain ring in Round 1.
2 All joins are slip stitches, unless otherwise indicated.
3 All new colors are joined with right side facing, unless otherwise indicated.
4 Weave in all ends as you go.
5 Standing stitches *(see Techniques)* can be used to start a round with a new color.
6 An invisible join *(see Techniques)* can be used at the end of a round to finish a color.
7 Blocking the finished project is recommended.

SPECIAL STITCHES

Join With Single Crochet (join with sc) - With slip knot on hook, insert hook into stitch or space indicated and pull up a loop (2 loops on hook). Yarn over and pull through both loops on hook (first single crochet made).

Double Treble (dtr): Yarn over hook three times, insert hook in stitch or space indicated and draw up a loop (five loops on hook). [Yarn over and pull yarn through two loops on hook] 4 times, until only one loop remains on hook.

Front Post Treble Crochet: (FPtr): Yarn over hook twice, insert hook from front to back to front around post of indicated stitch, yarn over and draw up a loop, [yarn over and pull through 2 loops on hook] 3 times (tr made).

Note: In this pattern, do NOT skip the stitch behind the FPtr.

Join-As-You-Go (jaygo): Drop loop from hook, insert hook from front to back through st or sp specified on previous motif, pick up dropped loop and pull through (join made).

CENTERPIECE

LARGE MOTIF (Make 7 – using specified colors)
ROUND 1: *(Right Side)* Starting with Color A, ch 4 join to first ch to form ring; ch 5 *(counts as first tr & ch-1)*, [tr in ring, ch 1] 11 times; join to first tr (4th ch of beg ch-5). (12 tr & 12 ch-1 sps) Fasten off Color A.

ROUND 2: Using Color B, **join with sc** *(see Special Stitches)* in any ch-1 sp, sc in same sp, ch 1, [2 sc in next ch-1 sp, ch 1] around; join to first sc. (24 sc & 12 ch-1 sps) Fasten off Color B.

ROUND 3: Join Color C with sl st to any ch-1 sp, ch 2, 2 hdc in same sp, ch 1, [2 hdc in next ch-1 sp, ch 1] around; join to first hdc. (24 hdc & 12 ch-1 sps) Fasten off Color C.

ROUND 4: Join Color A with sl st to any ch-1 sp, ch 2, hdc in same sp, ch 3, [hdc in next ch-1 sp, ch 3] around; join to first hdc. (12 hdc & 12 ch-3 sps) Fasten off Color A.

ROUND 5: Join Color C with sl st to any ch-3 sp, ch 3 *(counts as first dc, now and throughout)*, 3 dc in same sp, [4 dc in next ch-3 sp] around; join to first dc (3rd ch of beg ch-3). (48 dc) Fasten off Color C.

Note: When working in the back loops, I suggest working through the back loop together with the loop below the back loop (third loop). This makes the stitch more stable and doesn't leave any holes.

ROUND 6: Using Color B, join with sc to **back loop** of first dc of any 4-dc group, working in **back loops** only, hdc in next dc, 2 dc in next dc, (tr, **dtr** *(see Special Stitches)*) in next dc, (dtr, tr) in next dc, 2 dc in next dc, hdc in next dc, *sc in each of next 2 dc, hdc in next dc,

2 dc in next dc, (tr, dtr) in next dc, (dtr, tr) in next dc, 2 dc in next dc, hdc in next dc; rep from * around, ending with sc in last dc; join to first sc. (12 sc, 12 hdc, 24 dc, 12 tr & 12 dtr) Fasten off Color B.

Following Layout Diagram, join as you go as follows:

First Motif – no join

ROUND 7: Using Color A, join with sc to sp between any 2 dtr-sts, ch 2, sc in same sp, sc in each of next 6 sts (dtr, tr, 2 dc, hdc, sc), **FPtr** (see Special Stitches) in corresponding hdc in Rnd 4, sc in each of next 6 sts (sc, hdc, 2 dc, tr, dtr), *(sc, ch 2 sc) in next sp between dtr-sts, sc in each of next 6 sts, FPtr in corresponding hdc in Rnd 4, sc in each of next 6 sts; rep from * around; join to first sc. (84 sc, 6 FPtr & 6 ch-2 sps) Fasten off Color A.

Second Motif – one join

ROUND 7: Using Color A, join with sc to sp between any 2 dtr-sts, ch 1, **jaygo** (see Special Stitches) in any ch-2 sp on First Motif, working in current motif, sc in same sp (as first sc), sc in each of next 6 sts, FPtr in corresponding hdc in Rnd 4, sc in each of next 6 sts, *(sc, ch 2 sc) in next sp between dtr-sts, sc in each of next 6 sts, FPtr in corresponding hdc in Rnd 4, sc in each of next 6 sts; rep from * around; join to first sc. (84 sc, 6 FPtr & 6 ch-2 sps) Fasten off Color A.

Motifs 3, 4, 5 & 6 – two joins

ROUND 7: Using Color A, join with sc to sp between any 2 dtr-sts, ch 1, jaygo in corresponding ch-2 sp on First Motif, ch 1 (join made), ♥ working in current motif, sc in same sp (as first sc), sc in each of next 6 sts, FPtr in corresponding hdc in Rnd 4, sc in each of next 6 sts ♥, sc in sp between dtr-sts, ch 1, jaygo in corresponding ch-2 sp on previous motif, ch 1 (2nd join made), rep from ♥ to ♥ once, *(sc, ch 2, sc) in next sp between dtr-sts, sc in each of next 6 sts, FPtr in corresponding hdc in Rnd 4, sc in each of next 6 sts; rep from * around; join to first sc. (84 sc, 6 FPtr & 6 ch-2 sps) Fasten off Color A.

Last Motif – three joins

ROUND 7: Using Color A, join with sc to sp between any 2 dtr-sts, ch 1, jaygo in corresponding ch-2 sp on Second

Motif, ch 1 (join made), ♥working in current motif, sc in same sp (as first sc), sc in each of next 6 sts, FPtr in corresponding hdc in Rnd 4, sc in each of next 6 sts♥, sc in sp between dtr-sts, ch 1, jaygo in corresponding ch-2 sp on First Motif, ch 1 (2nd join made), rep from ♥ to ♥ once, sc in sp between dtr-sts, ch 1, jaygo in corresponding ch-2 sp on Sixth Motif, ch 1 (3rd join made), rep from ♥ to ♥ once, *(sc, ch 2, sc) in next sp between dtr-sts, sc in each of next 6 sts, FPtr in corresponding hdc in Rnd 4, sc in each of next 6 sts; rep from * around; join to first sc. (84 sc, 6 FPtr & 6 ch-2 sps) Fasten off Color A.

SMALL MOTIF – Make 12

ROUND 1: (Right Side) Starting with Color A, ch 4 join to first ch to form ring; ch 5 (counts as first tr & ch-1), [tr in ring, ch 1] 11 times; join to first tr (4th ch of beg ch-5). (12 tr & 12 ch-1 sps)

Following Layout Diagram, join as you go as follows:

Inner Motifs – 3 sided join (use 6 motifs)

ROUND 2: Ch 1, 3 sc in next ch-1 sp, *ch 2, jaygo in corresponding tr on Large Motif, ch 2, working in current motif, 3 sc in each of next 4 ch-1 sps; rep from * around, omitting last 3 sc on final repeat; join to first sc. (36 sc & 3 joins). Fasten off Color A.

Outer Motifs – 2 sided join (use 6 motifs)

ROUND 2: Ch 1, 3 sc in each of next 7 ch-1 sps, *ch 2, jaygo in corresponding tr on Large Motif, ch 2, working in current motif**, 3 sc in each of next 4 ch-1 sps; rep from * to **, 3 sc in last ch-1 sp; join to first sc. (36 sc & 2 joins). Fasten off Color A.

When complete, lightly block centerpiece.

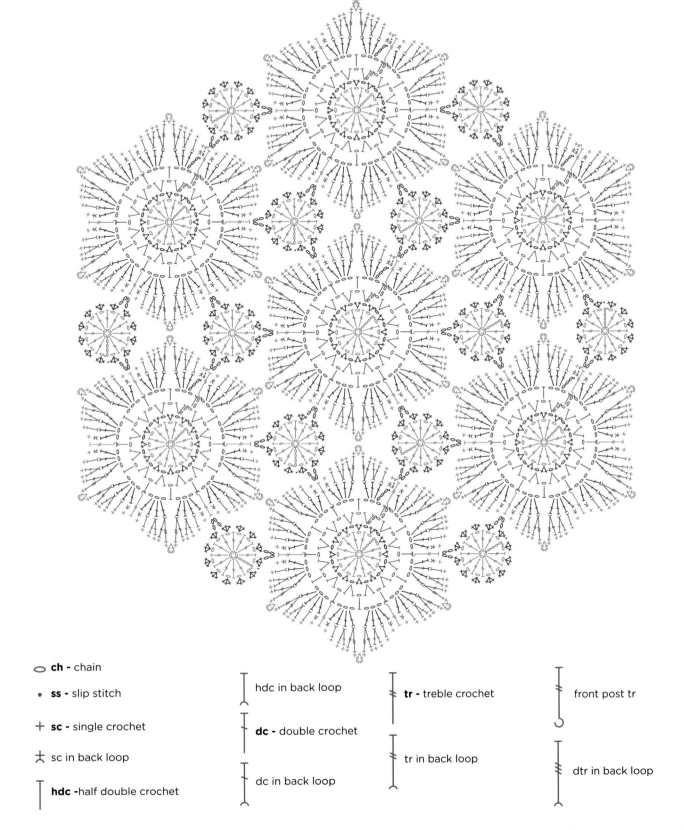

⬭ **ch -** chain	⊤ hdc in back loop	⧧ **tr -** treble crochet
• **ss -** slip stitch		
+ **sc -** single crochet	⊤ **dc -** double crochet	⧧ tr in back loop
⅄ sc in back loop		
⊤ **hdc -** half double crochet	⊤ dc in back loop	

front post tr

dtr in back loop

DANDELION
BOUQUET DOILY

I love how these blues work together. Add Amaranto and I am jumping up and down!
You will notice these colors make frequent appearances throughout the book as I love them
so much. This doily works up beautifully (and you may find my favorite stitch in there too).
This is the largest doily design in the book, making it a perfect piece to place on a side table
and add some color to a 'crochet corner'. We all have one or more of those, don't we?

Finished Size

About 15" (38 cm) diameter

FINISHED SIZE
About 15" (38 cm) diameter

MATERIALS

DMC Natura Just Cotton
  Color A – Ibiza (#01)
  Color B – Bleu Layette (#05)
  Color C – Blue Jeans (#26)
  Color D – Amaranto (#33)
One ball of each color was used for the pictured Doily.

Hook: Size E-4 (3.50 mm)

Scissors & Yarn Needle

PATTERN NOTES

1 A Magic Ring *(see Techniques)* can be used instead of the chain ring in Round 1.
2 All joins are slip stitches, unless otherwise indicated.
3 All new colors are joined with right side facing, unless otherwise indicated.
4 Weave in all ends as you go.
5 Standing stitches *(see Techniques)* can be used to start a round with a new color.
6 An invisible join *(see Techniques)* can be used at the end of a round to finish a color.
7 Lightly blocking the finished doily to an even circular shape is recommended.

SPECIAL STITCHES

Join With Single Crochet (join with sc) - With slip knot on hook, insert hook into stitch or space indicated and pull up a loop (2 loops on hook). Yarn over and pull through both loops on hook (first single crochet made).

Popcorn (pc): Work 5 dc in same stitch or space indicated, drop lp from hook, insert hook from front to back in first dc made, pull dropped lp through, ch 1 (to lock).

Picot: Chain 3, insert hook back into the center of the base stitch (through both the front loop and loop below the front loop), yarn over and pull through stitch and loops on hook (slip stitch made).

DOILY

ROUND 1: *(Right Side)* Starting with Color A, ch 4; join to first ch to form ring; ch 3 *(counts as first dc, now and throughout)*, 11 dc in ring; join to first dc *(3rd ch of beg ch-3)*. (12 dc) Fasten off Color A.

ROUND 2: Using Color B, **join with sc (see Special Stitches)** to any dc, ch 1, [sc in next dc, ch 1] around; join to first sc. (12 sc & 12 ch-1 sps) Fasten off Color B.

ROUND 3: Join Color C with sl st to any ch-1 sp, ch 2, 2 hdc in same sp, ch 1, [2 hdc in next ch-1 sp, ch 1] around; join to first hdc. (24 hdc & 12 ch-1 sps) Fasten off Color C.

ROUND 4: Join Color A with sl st to any ch-1 sp, ch 3, 2 dc in same sp, [3 dc in next ch-1 sp] around; join to first dc *(3rd ch of beg ch-3)*. (36 dc) Fasten off Color A.

ROUND 5: Join Color D with sl st to sp between any 3-dc group, ch 6 *(counts as first dc & ch-3)*, dc in same sp as joining, [(dc, ch 3, dc) in next sp between dc-groups] around; join to first dc *(3rd ch of beg ch-3)*. (24 dc & 12 ch-3 sps) Fasten off Color D.

ROUND 6: Join Color B with sl st to any ch-3 sp, ch 3, 5 dc in same sp, [6 dc in next ch-3 sp] around; join to first dc *(3rd ch of beg ch-3)*. (72 dc) Fasten off Color B.

ROUND 7: Join Color C with sl st to first dc of any 6-dc group, ch 4 *(counts as first dc, & ch-1)*, [skip next dc, dc in next dc, ch 1] twice, skip next dc, dc in next *(6th in group)* dc, *[dc in next dc, ch 1, skip next dc] 3 times, dc in next dc; rep from * around; join to first dc *(3rd ch of beg ch-3)*. (48 dc & 36 ch-1 sps) Fasten off Color C.

ROUND 8: Using Color A, join with sc to first dc made on Rnd 7, [sc in next st or sp] around; join to first sc. (84 sc) Fasten off Color A.

ROUND 9: Using Color D, join with sc to first sc made on Rnd 8, sc in each of next 2 sc, pc *(see Special Stitches)* in next (center of group) sc, [sc in each of next 6 sc, pc in next sc] around, ending with sc in each of last 3 sc; join to first sc. (72 sc & 12 pc)

ROUND 10: Join Color B with sl st to any pc, ch 6 *(counts as first tr & ch-2)*, tr in same st, ch 7, skip next 6 sc, [(tr, ch 2, tr) in next pc, ch 7, skip next 6 sc] around; join to first tr *(4th ch of beg ch-6)*. (24 tr, 12 ch-2 sps & 12 ch-6 lps)

ROUND 11: Sl st in next ch-2 sp, ch 3, 6 dc in same sp, ch 3, sc in ch-6 lp, ch 3, [7 dc in next ch-2 sp, ch 3, sc in next ch-6 lp, ch 3] around; join to first dc *(3rd ch of beg ch-3)*. (84 dc, 12 sc & 24 ch-3 sps) Fasten off Color B.

ROUND 12: Using Color C, join with sc to any sc, *ch 1, [dc in next dc, ch 1] 7 times, sc in next sc; rep from * around, omitting last sc on final repeat; join to first sc. (84 dc, 12 sc & 96 ch-1 sps) Fasten off Color C.

ROUND 13: Using Color D, join with sc to ch-1 sp after 2nd dc of any 7-dc fan, sc in same sp, 2 sc in next ch-1 sp, *picot *(see Special Stiches)*, 2 sc in each of next 2 ch-1 sps, ch 3, skip next 2 ch-1 sps, tr in next sc, picot, ch 3, skip next 2 ch-1 sps, 2 sc in each of next 2 ch-1 sps; repeat from * around, omitting last 2 sc on final repeat; join to first sc. (96 sc, 12 tr, 24 picots & 24 ch-3 sps) Fasten off Color D.

ROUND 14: Join Color A with sl st to ch-3 sp before any tr, ch 3, 3 dc in same sp, *hdc in picot, 4 dc in next ch-3 sp, ch 5, skip next 4 sc, sc in next picot, ch 5, skip next 4 sc, 4 dc in next ch-3 sp; rep from * around, omitting last 4 dc on final repeat; join to first dc *(3rd ch of beg ch-3)*. (96 dc, 12 hdc, 12 sc & 24 ch-5 lps) Fasten off Color A.

ROUND 15: Join Color B to second dc made on Rnd 14, ch 3, dc in each of next 2 dc, dc in next hdc, dc in each of next 3 dc, *ch 3, skip next dc, sc in next ch-5 lp, ch 3, skip next sc, sc in next ch-5 lp, ch 3, skip next dc**, dc in each of next 7 sts; rep from * around, ending at ** on final repeat; join to first dc *(3rd ch of beg ch-3)*. (84 dc, 24 sc & 36 ch-3 lps) Fasten off Color B.

ROUND 16: Join Color C to second dc made on Rnd 15, ch 3, dc in each of next 4 dc, *ch 3, skip next dc, [sc in next ch-3 lp, ch 3] 3 times, skip next dc**, dc in each of next 5 dc; rep from * around, ending at ** on final repeat; join to first dc *(3rd ch of beg ch-3)*. (60 dc, 36 sc & 48 ch-3 lps) Fasten off Color C.

ROUND 17: Join Color D to second dc made on Rnd 16, ch 3, dc in each of next 2 dc, *ch 3, skip next dc, [sc in next ch-3 lp, ch 3] 4 times, skip next dc**, dc in each of next 3 dc; rep from * around, ending at ** on final repeat; join to first dc *(3rd ch of beg ch-3)*. (36 dc, 48 sc & 60 ch-3 lps) Fasten off Color D.

ROUND 18: Join Color A with sl st to second *(center)* dc on Rnd 17, ch 3, 4 dc in same stitch as joining, drop lp from hook, insert hook from front to back in first dc made *(3rd ch of beg ch-3)*, pull dropped lp through *(first popcorn made)*, *ch 3, skip next dc, [sc in next ch-3 lp, ch 3] 5 times, skip next dc**, pc in next *(center)* dc; rep from * around, ending at ** on final repeat; join to first pc. (12 pc, 60 sc & 72 ch-3 lps) Fasten off Color A.

ROUND 19: Using Color B, join with sc to any ch-3 lp, ch 4, [sc in next ch-3 lp, ch 4] around; join to first sc. (72 sc & 72 ch-4 lps) Fasten off Color B.

ROUND 20: Using Color C, join with sc to any ch-4 lp, [ch 4, sc in next ch-4 lp] around, ending with ch 1; join with dc to first sc *(to form last ch-4 lp and positions yarn for next round)*. (72 sc & 72 ch-4 lps) Fasten off Color C.

ROUND 21: Ch 1, sc in ch-4 lp under hook, picot, ch 3, [sc in next ch-4 lp, picot, ch 3] around; join to first sc. (72 sc/picots & 72 ch-3 lps) Fasten off Color C.

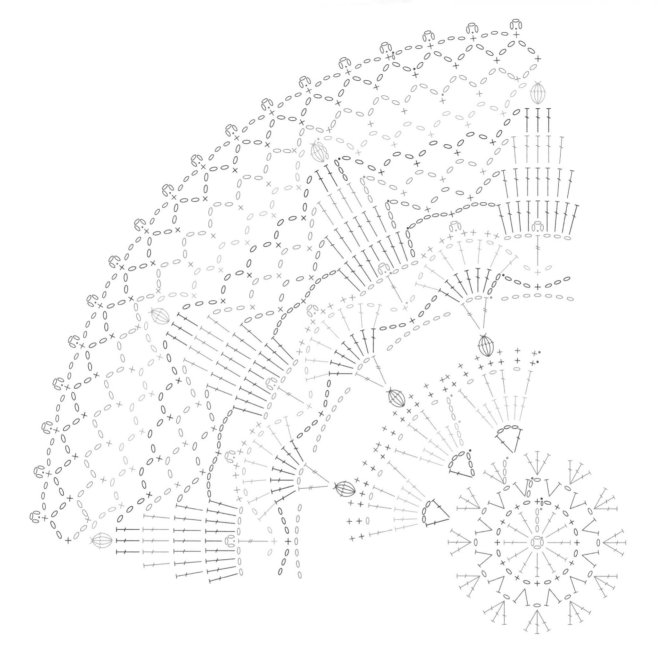

⬭ **ch -** chain	⊺ **hdc -** half double crochet	🪅 first 5-dc popcorn
• **ss -** slip stitch	⊥ **dc -** double crochet	🪅 5-dc popcorn
+ **sc -** single crochet	⧧ **tr -** treble crochet	
0̤.0 picot		

FENCED AROUND WALL HANGING

It's no secret that I adore using colors which blend nicely from one to the next. I love the effect it gives any piece of crochet. You will notice that throughout most of my designs I tend to do this. Then, I like to add a color that makes the entire piece either stand out or have a calming effect. In this particular design, I chose a shade of white to give it more detail and make it more eye-catching. By not attaching the hoop, this wall hanging becomes a gorgeous doily. Which is your preference…

A doily or a wall-hanging?

Finished Size

About 11½" (29 cm) diameter

FINISHED SIZE

About 11½" (29 cm) diameter

MATERIALS

DMC Natura Just Cotton

Color A – Ivory (#02)
Color B – Light Green (#12)
Color C – Aguamarine (#25)
Color D – Star Light (#27)

One ball of each color was used for the pictured Wall-hanging.

Hook: Size E-4 (3.50 mm)

Scissors & Yarn Needle

12" (30 cm) (Macramé) Ring

PATTERN NOTES

1 All joins are slip stitches, unless otherwise indicated.
2 All new colors are joined with right side facing, unless otherwise indicated.
3 Weave in all ends as you go.
4 Standing stitches *(see Techniques)* can be used to start a round with a new color.
5 An invisible join *(see Techniques)* can be used at the end of a round to finish a color.

SPECIAL STITCHES

Cluster (cl): Yarn over, insert hook in stitch or space indicated and draw up a loop (3 loops on hook), yarn over, pull through 2 loops on hook (2 loops on remain on hook), yarn over, insert hook in same stitch or space and draw up a loop, yarn over, pull through 2 loops on hook (3 loops remain on hook), yarn over, pull through all 3 loops on hook.

Front Post Treble Crochet: (FPtr): Yarn over hook twice, insert hook from front to back to front around post of indicated stitch, yarn over and draw up a loop, [yarn over and pull through 2 loops on hook] 3 times (tr made). *Unless noted otherwise, always skip the st behind the FPtr.*

WALL-HANGING

ROUND 1: (Right Side) Using Color A, ch 8, join with sl st to first ch to form ring; ch 1, 12 sc in ring; join to first sc. (12 sc)

ROUND 2: Ch 2, dc in same st as joining (first cluster made), ch 2, [**cl** *(see Special Stitches)* in next sc, ch 2] around; join to first dc. (12 clusters & 12 ch-2 sps) Fasten off Color A.

ROUND 3: Using Color B, **join with sc** *(see Special Stitches)* to any ch-2 sp, 2 sc in same sp, [3 sc in next ch-2 sp] around; join to first sc. (36 sc) Fasten off Color B.

ROUND 4: Join Color C with sl st to any sc, ch 3 *(counts as first dc, now and throughout)*, dc in same st as joining, dc in each of next 2 sc, [2 dc in next sc, dc in each of next 2 sc] around; join to first dc *(3rd ch of beg ch-3)*. (48 dc)

ROUND 5: Join Color D with sl st to first dc of any 2-dc group, ch 2, dc in same st as joining *(first cluster made)*, ch 2, skip next dc, [cl in next dc, ch 2, skip next dc] around; join to first dc. (24 clusters & 24 ch-2 sps) Fasten off Color D.

ROUND 6: Using Color A, join with sc to any ch-2 sp, 2 sc in same sp, [3 sc in next ch-2 sp] around; join to first sc. (72 sc) Fasten off Color A.

ROUND 7: Join Color B with sl st to first sc of any 3-sc group, ch 3, dc in same st as joining, dc in each of next 2 sc, [2 dc in next sc, dc in each of next 2 sc] around; join to first dc *(3rd ch of beg ch-3)*. (96 dc) Fasten off Color B.

ROUND 8: Join Color C with sl st to first dc of any 2-dc group, ch 2, dc in same st as joining *(first cluster made)*, ch 4, skip next 3 dc, [cl in next dc, ch 4, skip next 3 dc] around; join to first dc. (24 clusters & 24 ch-4 sps) Fasten off Color C.

ROUND 9: Using Color D, join with sc to any ch-4 sp, 4 sc in same sp, [5 sc in next ch-4 sp] around; join to first sc. (120 sc) Fasten off Color D.

ROUND 10: Join Color A with sl st to first sc of any 5-sc group, ch 3, dc in same st as joining, dc in each of next 4 sc, [2 dc in next sc, dc in each of next 4 sc] around; join to first dc (3*rd* ch of beg ch-3). (144 dc) Fasten off Color A.

ROUND 11: Join Color B with sl st to first dc of any 2-dc group, ch 2, dc in same st as joining (first cluster made), ch 2, skip next 2 dc, [cl in next dc, ch 2, skip next 2 dc] around; join to first dc. (48 clusters & 48 ch-4 sps) Fasten off Color B.

ROUND 12: Using Color C, join with sc to any ch-2 sp, 2 sc in same sp, [3 sc in next ch-2 sp] around; join to first sc. (144 sc) Fasten off Color C.

ROUND 13: Join Color D with sl st to first sc of any 3-sc group, ch 3, dc in same st as joining, dc in each of next 5 sc, [2 dc in next sc, dc in each of next 5 sc] around; join to first dc (3*rd* ch of beg ch-3). (168 dc) Fasten off Color D.

ROUND 14: Using Color A, join with sc to dc after any 2-dc group, sc in each of next 5 dc, **FPtr** (see Special Stitches) in corresponding cl on Rnd 11, [sc in each of next 6 dc, FPtr in next cl on Rnd 11] around; join to first sc. (144 sc & 24 tr) Fasten off Color A.

ROUND 15: Join Color B with sl st to any tr, ch 2, dc in same st as joining (first cluster made), *[ch 2, cl] twice in same st, ch 1, skip next 2 sc, sc in each of next 2 sc, ch 1, skip next 2 sc**, cl in next tr; rep from * around, ending at ** on final repeat; join to first dc. (72 clusters, 48 sc, 48 ch-2 sps & 48 ch-1 sps) Fasten off Color B.

ROUND 16: Using Color D, join with sc to first cl of any 3-cl group, *2 sc in next ch-2 sp, (sc, ch 1, sc) in next (center) cl, 2 sc in next ch-2 sp, sc in next cl, sc in next ch-1 sp, skip next 2 sc, sc in next ch-1 sp**, sc in next cl; rep from * around, ending at ** on final repeat; join to first sc. (240 sc & 24 ch-1 sps) Fasten off Color D.

FINISHING WALL-HANGING – Use photo as guide
With right side facing, stretch piece slightly to fit in ring. Using a strand of Color D and yarn needle, whipstitch through ch-1 sps on last round over macramé ring. Secure and fasten off, weaving in ends.

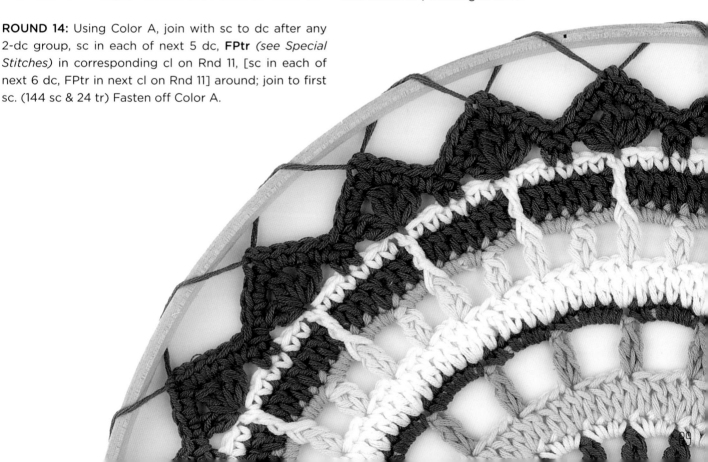

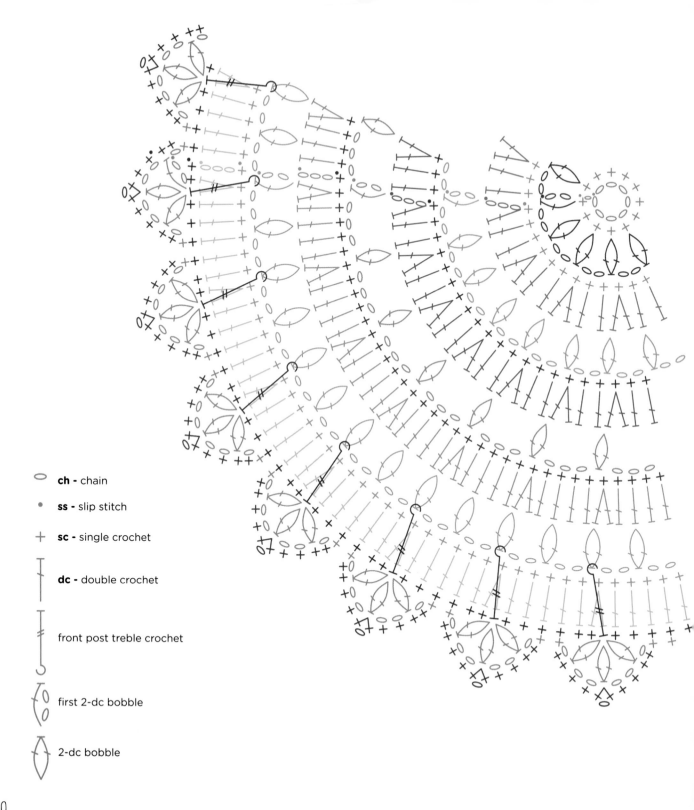

ⵔ **ch -** chain

• **ss -** slip stitch

✛ **sc -** single crochet

⊤ **dc -** double crochet

front post treble crochet

first 2-dc bobble

2-dc bobble

LOOPING AROUND GARLAND

I love the look of crocheted garlands. The way they softly drape, the way your eyes follow each motif as you gaze upon their beauty. This particular garland isn't as dainty-looking as 'Spotty & Dotty' (on page 86 in this book), due to the join-as-you-go method. This is another design you can modify and make the garland as long or as short as desired. Have fun playing around with vibrant colors, or perhaps keep to those cool and calming natural tones. Go ahead - make whatever tickles your fancy.

Finished Size

Each motif - About 3½"
(9 cm) diameter

FINISHED SIZE
Each motif - About 3½" (9 cm) diameter

MATERIALS

DMC Natura Just Cotton
Main Color - Ivory (#02)
Pink Colors
    Rose Layette (#06)
    Spring Rose (#07)
    Amaranto (#33)
Blue Colors
    Bleu Layette (#05)
    Blue Jeans (#26)
    Star Light (#27)
Colors used in random order in motifs. One ball of each color made a garland of 18 motifs – 9 Pink & 9 Blue.

Hook: Size E-4 (3.50 mm)

Scissors & Yarn Needle

PATTERN NOTES

1 A Magic Ring *(see Techniques)* can be used instead of the chain ring in Round 1.
2 All joins are slip stitches, unless otherwise indicated.
3 All new colors are joined with right side facing, unless otherwise indicated.
4 Weave in all ends as you go.
5 Standing stitches *(see Techniques)* can be used to start a round with a new color.
6 An invisible join *(see Techniques)* can be used at the end of a round to finish a color.

MOTIF

ROUND 1: *(Right Side)* Starting with first color, ch 4 join to first ch to form ring; ch 4 (counts as first tr), tr in ring, ch 4, [2 tr in ring, ch 4] 5 times; join to first tr. *(4ᵗʰ ch of beg ch-4)* (12 tr & 6 ch-4 lps) Fasten off.

ROUND 2: Join next color with sl st to any ch-4 lp, ch 3 *(counts as first dc, now and throughout)*, 4 dc in same lp, ch 2, [5 dc in next ch-4 lp, ch 2] around; join to first dc *(3ʳᵈ ch of beg ch-3)*. (30 dc & 6 ch-2 sps) Fasten off.

ROUND 3: Using next color, join with sc to third *(center)* dc of any 5-dc group, sc in each of next 2 dc, 3 sc in next ch-2 sp, [sc in each of next 5 dc, 3 sc in next ch-2 sp] around, ending with sc in each of next 2 dc; join to first sc. (48 sc) Fasten off.

GARLAND

Make as many motifs as you require, in color combinations of your choice.

JOINING ROUND: Starting with first motif, using Main Color, join with sl st to any sc worked into the center dc of Rnd 2, ch 3, *dc in each of next 3 sc, [2 dc in next sc, dc in each of next 3 sc] 5 times**, dc in next sc, ch 1; *(leave rem 23 sts unworked)*, pick up next motif, dc in any sc worked into the center dc of Rnd 2; rep from * across all motifs, ending at ** on last motif, continuing around motif, [2 dc in next sc, dc in each of next 3 sc] 6 times, ♥dc in next sc (same sc as first dc); sl st in first dc (of this motif) ♥♥, sl st in ch-1 sp between motifs, sl st in last dc worked on next motif, dc in same sc as last dc, dc in each of next 3 sc, [2 dc in next sc, dc in each of next 3 sc] 5 times; rep from ♥ across motifs, ending at ♥♥ on final repeat. (Each Motif has 60 dc) Fasten off Main Color.

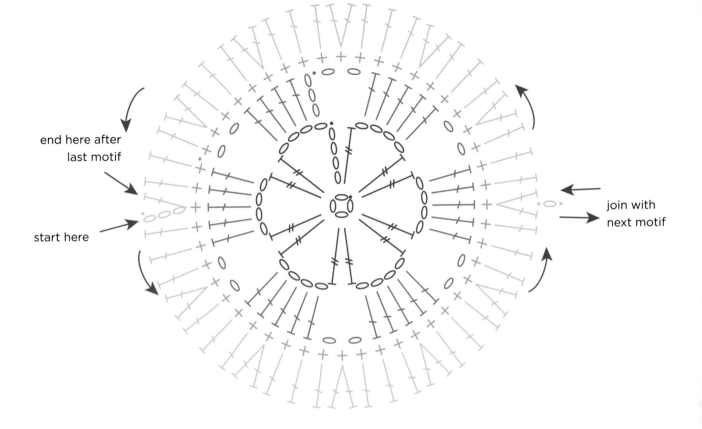

end here after
last motif

start here

join with
next motif

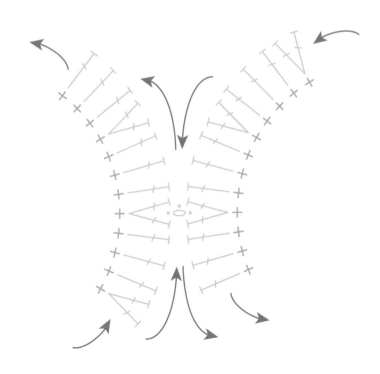

⬯ **ch -** chain

• **ss -** slip stitch

✚ **sc -** single crochet

🅣 **dc -** double crochet

🅣 **tr -** treble crochet

FLOWER PETALS CUSHION

Who doesn't like a chunky round cushion? I love how quickly this took to make up. The two sides are exactly the same which makes this a nice and easy pattern to follow. You could change it up by using different colors for each round. Naturally, I went with my trusty favorite color of green. I love all shades of greens, teals, aquas, etc.. I find them soothing and inviting. The instructions are included to make the round pillow form, in case you can't find a 20" round pillow.

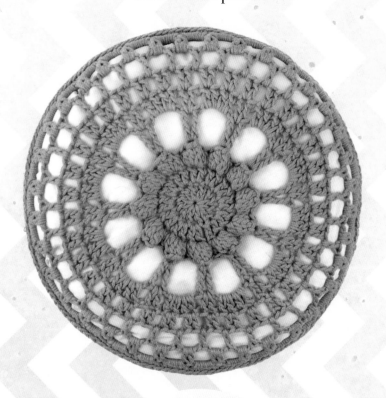

Finished Size

About 20" (51 cm) diameter

FINISHED SIZE

About 20" (51 cm) diameter

MATERIALS

DMC Natura Just Cotton XL

Lagoon (#07) 3 balls

Hook: Size K-10½ (6.50 mm)

Scissors & Yarn Needle

20" Round pillow form

PATTERN NOTES

1 A Magic Ring *(see Techniques)* can be used instead of the chain ring in Round 1.
2 All joins are slip stitches, unless otherwise indicated.
3 All new colors are joined with right side facing, unless otherwise indicated.
4 Weave in all ends as you go.
5 Standing stitches *(see Techniques)* can be used to start a round with a new color.
6 An invisible join *(see Techniques)* can be used at the end of a round to finish a color.
7 Blocking the finished sides is recommended before joining together.

SPECIAL STITCHES

Popcorn (pc): Work 5 dc in same stitch or space indicated, drop lp from hook, insert hook from front to back in first dc made, pull dropped lp through.

Cluster (cl): Yarn over, insert hook in stitch or space indicated and draw up a loop (3 loops on hook), yarn over, pull through 2 loops on hook (2 loops on remain on hook), yarn over, insert hook in same stitch or space and draw up a loop, yarn over, pull through 2 loops on hook (3 loops remain on hook), yarn over, pull through all 3 loops on hook.

Join With Single Crochet (join with sc) - With slip knot on hook, insert hook into stitch or space indicated and pull up a loop (2 loops on hook). Yarn over and pull through both loops on hook (first single crochet made).

CUSHION COVER SIDE – Make 2

ROUND 1: *(Right Side)* With Main Color, ch 4; join to first ch to form ring; ch 3 (counts as first dc, now and throughout), 11 dc in ring; join to first dc *(3rd ch of beg ch-3)*. (12 dc)

ROUND 2: Ch 3, dc in same st as joining, [2 dc in next dc] around; join to first dc *(3rd ch of beg ch-3)*. (24 dc)

ROUND 3: Ch 2 *(does NOT count as first hdc)*, 2 hdc in same st as joining, **pc** *(see Special Stitches)* in next dc, [2 hdc in next dc, pc in next dc] around; join to first hdc. (24 hdc & 12 popcorn)

ROUND 4: Sl st in next pc, ch 4 *(counts as first tr)*, tr in same st, ch 4, skip next 2 hdc, [2 tr in next pc, ch 4, skip next 2 hdc] around; join to first tr *(4th ch of beg ch-4)*. (24 tr & 12 ch-4 lps)

ROUND 5: Sl st in sp between tr-sts, ch 3, dc in same sp, *skip next tr, 4 dc in next ch-4 sp, skip next tr**, 2 dc in sp between tr-sts; rep from * around, ending at ** on final repeat; join to first dc *(3rd ch of beg ch-3)*. (72 dc)

ROUND 6: Sl st in next dc, ch 3, dc in same st, ch 1, skip next dc, [2 dc in next dc, ch 1, skip next dc] around; join to first dc *(3rd ch of beg ch-3)*. (72 dc & 36 ch-1 sps)

ROUND 7: Sl st in next ch-1 sp, ch 6 *(counts as first dc & ch-3)*, skip next 2 dc, [dc in next ch-1 sp, ch 3] around; join to first dc *(3rd ch of beg ch-6)*. (36 dc & 36 ch-3 sps)

ROUND 8: Sl st in next ch-3 sp, ch 2, dc in same sp *(first cluster made)*, ch 3, [**cl** *(see Special Stitches)* in next ch-3 sp, ch 3] around; join to first dc. (36 clusters & 36 ch-3 sps)

ROUND 9: Sl st to next ch-3 sp, ch 2, 4 dc in same sp, [4 dc in next ch-3 sp] around; join to first dc. (144 dc) Fasten off and weave in all ends.

ASSEMBLY OF CUSHION COVER – Use photo as guide

With right sides of both Sides facing *(wrong sides together)*, working through both thicknesses and matching sts, using Main Color, **join with sc** *(see Special Stitches)* to any dc, [sc in next dc] around, inserting pillow form about half-way through; join to first sc. (144 sc) Fasten off and weave in all ends.

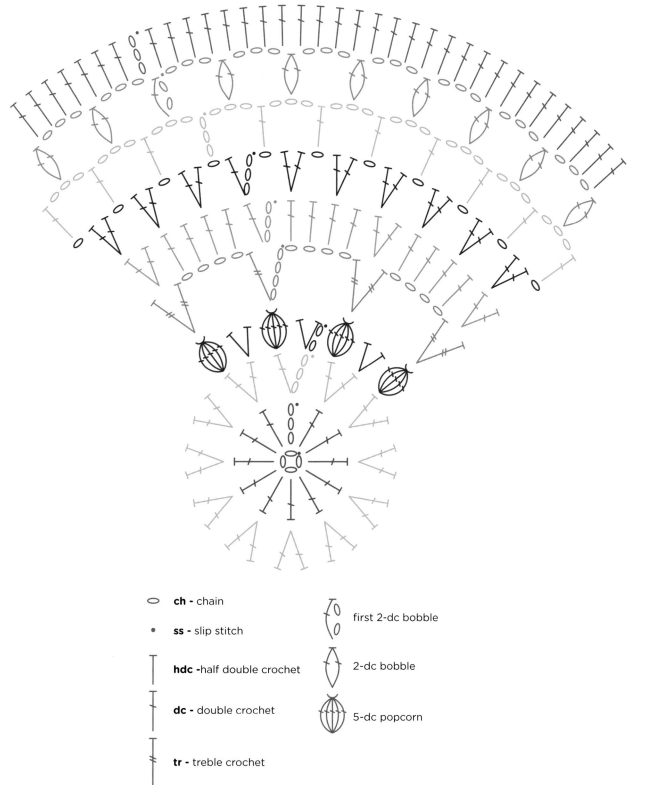

ch - chain

ss - slip stitch

hdc - half double crochet

dc - double crochet

tr - treble crochet

first 2-dc bobble

2-dc bobble

5-dc popcorn

LAZY DAISY SHOULDER BAG

In the past, making crocheted bags wasn't high on my project list of things-to-do. That's all changed now! I had such fun designing and making this little treasure. It is a quick to make using the chunky yarn. I even learned how to make a twisted braid for the handle.

Finished Size

About 9 ½" (24 cm) diameter

FINISHED SIZE

About 9 ½" (24 cm) diameter
Cord Handle (before joining) – about 36" (92 cm) long
Height of Bag (with handle) – about 27 ½" long

MATERIALS

DMC Natura Just Cotton XL

> Color A – Grey Green (#72)
> Color B – Ecru (#03)
> Color C – Acanthus (#42)

One ball of each color used to make Bag.

Hook: Size K-10 ½ (6.50 mm)

Scissors & Yarn Needle

PATTERN NOTES

1 A Magic Ring (see Techniques) can be used instead of the chain ring in Round 1.
2 All joins are slip stitches, unless otherwise indicated.
3 All new colors are joined with right side facing, unless otherwise indicated.
4 Weave in all ends as you go.
5 Standing stitches (see Techniques) can be used to start a round with a new color.
6 An invisible join (see Techniques) can be used at the end of a round to finish a color.
7 Blocking of finished Sides is recommended before joining together.

SPECIAL STITCHES

Join With Single Crochet (join with sc): With slip knot on hook, insert hook into stitch or space indicated and pull up a loop (2 loops on hook). Yarn over and pull through both loops on hook (first single crochet made).

Front Post Treble Crochet (FPtr): Yarn over hook twice, insert hook from front to back to front around post of indicated stitch, yarn over and draw up a loop, [yarn over and pull through 2 loops on hook] 3 times (tr made).

Reverse Single Crochet (or Crab Stitch) (rev-sc): With a loop on the hook, * insert hook in next st to the right and pull up loop, yarn over and pull through both loops on hook. Repeat from * across (or around).

SHOULDER BAG

BAG SIDE – Make 2

ROUND 1: *(Right Side)* Starting with Color A, ch 4; join to first ch to form ring; ch 3 *(counts as first dc, now and throughout)*, 11 dc in ring; join to first dc *(3rd ch of beg ch-3)*. (12 dc) Fasten off Color A.

ROUND 2: Join Color B with sl st to any dc, ch 4 *(counts as first tr)*, tr in same st as joining, ch 1, [2 tr in next dc, ch 1] around; join to first tr *(4th ch of beg ch-4)*. (24 tr & 12 ch-1 sps) Fasten off Color B.

ROUND 3: Join Color A with sl st to any ch-1 sp, ch 2 *(does NOT count as first hdc)*, 2 hdc in same sp, ch 2, [2 hdc in next ch-1 sp, ch 2] around; join to first hdc. (24 hdc & 12 ch-2 sps) Fasten off Color A.

ROUND 4: Using Color C, **join with sc** *(see Special Stitches)* to second hdc of any 2-hdc-group, 2 sc in same st, ch 2, skip next ch-sp, skip next hdc, [3 sc in next (2nd) hdc, ch 2] around; join to first sc. (36 sc & 12 ch-2 sps) Fasten off Color C.

Note: When working in the back loops, I suggest working through the back loop together with the loop below the back loop (third loop). This makes the stitch more stable and doesn't leave any holes.

ROUND 5: Using Color B, join with sc to **back loop** of first sc of any 3-sc group, working in **back loops** only, 2 sc in next sc, sc in next sc, **FPtr** *(see Special Stitches)* in each of next 2 corresponding tr of Rnd 2, *sc in next sc, 2 sc in next sc, sc in next sc, FPtr in each of next 2 corresponding tr of Rnd 2; rep from * around; join to first sc. (48 sc & 24 tr) Fasten off Color B.

ROUND 6: Using Color A, join with sc to **back loop** of first sc of any 4-sc group, working in **back loops** only, sc in each of next 3 sc, ch 2, skip next 2 tr, [sc in each of next 4 sc, ch 2, skip next 2 tr] around; join to first sc. (48 sc & 12 ch-2 sps) Fasten off Color A.

ROUND 7: Using Color C, join with sc to any ch-2 sp, sc in same sp, working in **back loops** only, sc in each of next 4 sc, [2 sc in next ch-2 sp, sc in each of next 4 sc] around; join to first sc. (72 sc) Fasten off Color C.

ROUND 8: Using Color A, join with sc to **back loop** of first sc of any 2-sc group (worked in ch-sp), working in **back loops** only, sc in next (second) sc (mark this sc on one Side), [sc in next sc] around; join to first sc. (72 sc) Fasten off Color A

CORD HANDLE

Using Color B, cut 12 strands of yarn, 6 times longer than needed for a comfortable strap. (I found that 16" (40 cm) was a good length for me, so my strands were each 96" (240 cm) long.

Knot the strands together at each end. Insert a pencil through half the strands at one end. Pin or tape the other end securely.

Fold yarn in half, keeping it taut to avoid tangling and remove pencil.

Insert knotted end into purse on other side of opening and gently push the knot through the stitches about an inch (2.5 cm) down.

ASSEMBLY OF BAG – Use photo as guide

With right sides of both Sides facing (wrong sides together) and Side with marked stitch facing, working through both thicknesses, matching stiches, using Color

A, join with sc to marked sc (together with the sc on other Side), **rev-sc** (see Special Stitches) in each of next 55 sc. Leave rem sts unworked. Fasten off and weave in all ends.

Keeping the yarn full length and taut, twist the pencil until the yarn is tightly twisted and when the tension is relaxed, it starts winding itself up.

Insert folded (unknotted) end into purse opening and out about an inch (2.5 cm) from start of rev-sc. Thread knotted end through fold and tug tightly.

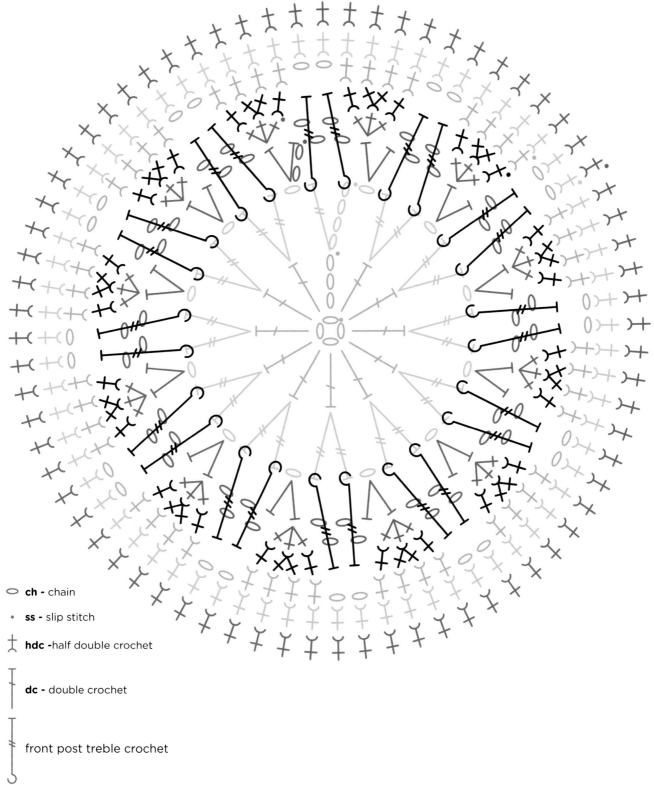

○ **ch -** chain

• **ss -** slip stitch

‡ **hdc -** half double crochet

† **dc -** double crochet

front post treble crochet

STRING OF BLOSSOMS TABLE RUNNER

For this design, I wanted something that had different sized motifs, like those amazing tablecloths our great-grandmothers made. However, I wanted something with more of a modern look and twist to it. If you're like me, and get bored after making the same thing over and over, the join-as-you-go method is a great technique. I love seeing a design grow as you progress, instead of making lots of motifs and then joining them all together. Besides making a beautiful table-runner, you can use adapt this design to make a centerpiece, a lovely shawl, either a blanket or a throw, and even a stunning cushion cover. The options are entirely up to you.

Finished Size

Large Motifs – About 4 ¼"
(11 cm) square

Small Motifs – About 2 ¼"
(6 cm) square

FINISHED SIZES

Large Motifs – About 4 ¼" (11 cm) square
Small Motifs – About 2 ¼" (6 cm) square

MATERIALS

DMC Natura Just Cotton
Colors Used – Blue Jeans (#26)
Glacier (#87)
Acanthe (#81)
Lobelia (#82)
Spring Rose (#07)
*One ball of each color made a table-runner with 18
Large and 8 Small motifs.*

Hook: Size E-4 (3.50 mm)

Scissors & Yarn Needle

PATTERN NOTES

1 A Magic Ring (see Techniques) can be used instead of
the chain ring in Round 1.
2 All joins are slip stitches, unless otherwise indicated.
3 All new colors are joined with right side facing, unless
otherwise indicated.
4 Weave in all ends as you go.
5 Standing stitches (see Techniques) can be used to
start a round with a new color.
6 An invisible join (see Techniques) can be used at the
end of a round to finish a color.
7 Blocking the finished project is recommended.

SPECIAL STITCHES

Join With Single Crochet (join with sc): With slip knot
on hook, insert hook into stitch or space indicated and
pull up a loop (2 loops on hook). Yarn over and pull
through both loops on hook (first single crochet made).

Three-Chain Picot (p3): Chain 3, insert hook back into
the center of the base stitch (through both the front
loop and loop below the front loop), yarn over and pull
through stitch and loops on hook (slip stitch made).

Join-As-You-Go (jaygo): Drop loop from hook, insert
hook from front to back through st or sp specified on
previous motif, pick up dropped loop and pull through
(join made).

TABLE-RUNNER

**LARGE MOTIF – Make 18 (or any even number), using
random colors of choice.**

ROUND 1: *(Right Side)* Starting with first color, ch 4 join
to first ch to form ring; ch 3 *(counts as first dc, now and
throughout)*, [dc in ring] 11 times; join to first dc (3rd ch of
beg ch-3). (12 dc) Fasten off.

ROUND 2: Using next color, **join with sc** *(see Special
Stitches)* to any dc, (sc, **p3** *(see Special Stitches)*, sc) in
next dc, [sc in each of next 2 dc, (sc, p3, sc) in next dc]
around, ending with sc in last dc; join to first sc. (16 sc &
4 picots) Fasten off.

ROUND 3: Join next color with sl st to first sc, ch 3, dc in
next sc, ch 9, skip picot, [dc in each of next 4 sc, ch 9]
around, ending with dc in each of last 2 sc; join to first dc
(3rd ch of beg ch-3). (16 dc & 4 ch-9 lps)

First Large Motif – no join

ROUND 4: Ch 1, sc in same st as joining, *skip next dc,
(sc, hdc, 4 dc, tr, ch 2, tr, 4 dc, hdc, sc) in next ch-9 lp,
skip next dc, sc in next dc, p3**, sc in next dc; rep from
* around, ending at ** on final repeat; join to first sc. (8
petals, 8 sc, 4 picots & 4 corner ch-2 sps) Fasten off.

Second Motif – one join

ROUND 4: Following Layout Diagram, ch 1, sc in same st
as joining, skip next dc, (sc, hdc, 4 dc, tr) in next ch-9 lp,
ch 1, **jaygo** *(see Special Stitches)* in any ch-2 sp on First
Motif, ch1, (tr, 4 dc, hdc, sc) in same ch-9 lp, skip next dc,
sc in next dc, p3, sc in next dc, *skip next dc, (sc, hdc,
4 dc, tr, ch 2, tr, 4 dc, hdc, sc) in next ch-9 lp, skip next
dc, sc in next dc, p3**, sc in next dc; rep from * around,
ending at ** on final repeat; join to first sc. (8 petals, 8 sc,
4 picots & 4 corner ch-2 sps) Fasten off.

Odd-Numbered Motifs (3, 5, 7, etc.) – one join

ROUND 4: Following Layout Diagram, ch 1, sc in same st as joining, skip next dc, (sc, hdc, 4 dc, tr) in next ch-9 lp, ch 1, jaygo in corresponding ch-2 sp of next to last Motif, ch1, (tr, 4 dc, hdc, sc) in same ch-9 lp, skip next dc, sc in next dc, p3, sc in next dc, *skip next dc, (sc, hdc, 4 dc, tr, ch 2, tr, 4 dc, hdc, sc) in next ch-9 lp, skip next dc, sc in next dc, p3**, sc in next dc; rep from * around, ending at ** on final repeat; join to first sc. (8 petals, 8 sc, 4 picots & 4 corner ch-2 sps) Fasten off.

Even-Numbered Motifs (4, 6, 8, etc.) – two joins

ROUND 4: Following Layout Diagram, ch 1, sc in same st as joining, skip next dc, (sc, hdc, 4 dc, tr) in next ch-9 lp, ch 1, jaygo in corresponding ch-2 sp of next to last Motif, ch1, (tr, 4 dc, hdc, sc) in same ch-9 lp, skip next dc, sc in next dc, p3, sc in next dc, skip next dc, (sc, hdc, 4 dc, tr) in next ch-9 lp, ch 1, jaygo in corresponding ch-2 sp of previous Motif, ch1, (tr, 4 dc, hdc, sc) in same ch-9 lp, skip next dc, sc in next dc, p3, sc in next dc, *skip next dc, (sc, hdc, 4 dc, tr, ch 2, tr, 4 dc, hdc, sc) in next ch-9 lp, skip next dc, sc in next dc, p3**, sc in next dc; rep from * around, ending at ** on final repeat; join to first sc. (8 petals, 8 sc, 4 picots & 4 corner ch-2 sps) Fasten off.

SMALL MOTIF – Make 10 (or half the number of Large Motifs made, plus one) using random colors of choice.

Note: These motifs are joined between four Large Motifs.

ROUNDS 1-2: Repeat Rnds 1-2 of Large Motif.
ROUND 3: Join next color with sl st to first sc, ch 3, dc in next sc, ch 4, skip picot, [dc in each of next 4 sc, ch 4] around, ending with dc in each of last 2 sc; join to first dc (*3rd ch of beg ch-3*). (16 dc & 4 ch-4 lps)

ROUND 4: Following Layout Diagram, ch 1, sc in same st as joining, *skip next dc, (sc, hdc, dc) in next ch-4 lp, ch 1, jaygo in picot of corresponding Large Motif, ch1, (dc, hdc, sc) in same ch-4 lp, skip next dc, sc in next dc, p3**,

sc in next dc; rep from * around, ending at ** on final repeat; join to first sc. (4 joined corners, 8 sc, 4 picots) Fasten off.

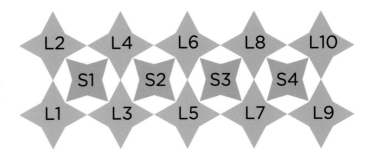

Main motif (outer)

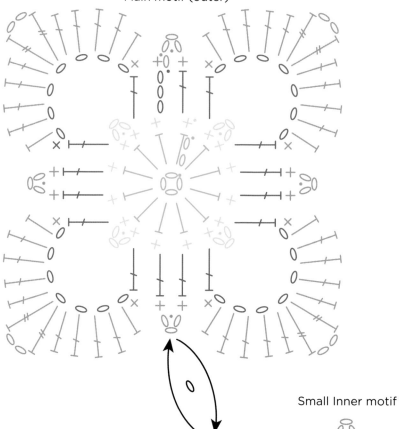

Small Inner motif

⬭ **ch -** chain

• **ss -** slip stitch

+ **sc -** single crochet

picot

hdc - half double crochet

dc - double crochet

tr - treble crochet

SPOTTY AND DOTTY GARLAND

The Spotty & Dotty Garland was the second design I came up with and made for this book. I knew I wanted at least one garland - and now we have two!

I love the effect created by using different sized motifs and the stitches used give this particular garland has a daintier look about it. You can tailor-make this garland to any length you like.

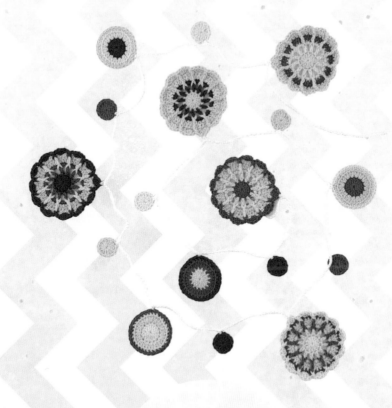

Finished Size

Large Motifs – About 3 ½"
(9 cm) diameter

FINISHED SIZE
Large Motifs – About 3 ½" (9 cm) diameter

MATERIALS

DMC Natura Just Cotton
Main Color – Ibiza (#01)
Colors Used – Bleu Layette (#05)
Ble (#83)
Glacier (#87)
Cerise (#62)
Star Light (#27)
One ball of each color made a garland with 5 Large, 4 Medium & 8 Small motifs.

Hook: Size E-4 (3.50 mm)

Scissors & Yarn Needle

PATTERN NOTES

1 A Magic Ring (see Techniques) can be used instead of the chain ring in Round 1.
2 All joins are slip stitches, unless otherwise indicated.
3 All new colors are joined with right side facing, unless otherwise indicated.
4 Weave in all ends as you go.
5 Standing stitches (see Techniques) can be used to start a round with a new color.
6 An invisible join (see Techniques) can be used at the end of a round to finish a color.

SPECIAL STITCHES

Join With Single Crochet (join with sc): With slip knot on hook, insert hook into stitch or space indicated and pull up a loop (2 loops on hook). Yarn over and pull through both loops on hook (first single crochet made).

Front Post Single Crochet: (FPsc): Insert hook from front to back to front around post of indicated stitch, yarn over and draw up a loop (2 loops on hook), yarn over and pull through both loops on hook. (single crochet made).
Unless noted otherwise, always skip the st behind the FPsc.

Front Post Treble Crochet: (FPtr): Yarn over hook twice, insert hook from front to back to front around post of indicated stitch, yarn over and draw up a loop, [yarn over and pull through 2 loops on hook] 3 times (treble made).
Unless noted otherwise, always skip the st behind the FPtr.

GARLAND

LARGE MOTIF – Make 5 (or any number) using random colors of choice.

ROUND 1: *(Right Side)* Starting with first color, ch 4 join to first ch to form ring; ch 3 (counts as first dc, now and throughout), [dc in ring] 11 times; join to first dc *(3rd ch of beg ch-3).* (12 dc) Fasten off.

ROUND 2: Join next color with sl st to any dc, ch 5 *(counts as first dc & ch-2),* [dc in next dc, ch 2] around; join to first dc. (12 dc & 12 ch-2 sps)

ROUND 3: Ch 1, [3 sc in next ch-2 sp] around; join to first sc. (36 sc) Fasten off.

ROUND 4: Join next color with sl st in first sc of any 3-sc group, ch 2, hdc in same st as joining, hdc in next sc, 2 hdc in next sc, [hdc in each of next 2 sc, 2 hdc in next sc] around; join to first hdc. (48 hdc) Fasten off.

ROUND 5: With next color, **join with sc** *(see Special Stitches)* to second hdc made in previous round, sc in next hdc, **FPtr** *(see Special Stitches)* in corresponding dc on Rnd 2, [sc in each of next 3 hdc, FPtr in corresponding dc on Rnd 2] around; join to first sc. (36 sc & 12 tr) Fasten off.

ROUND 6: Join next color with sl st to center sc of any 3-sc group, ch 2, 3 hdc in same st as joining, ch 1, skip next sc, **FPsc** *(see Special Stitches)* in next tr, ch 1, skip next sc, [3 hdc in next sc, ch 1, skip next sc, FPsc in next tr, ch 1, skip next sc] around; join to first hdc. (36 hdc, 12 sc & 24 ch-1 sps) Fasten off.

MEDIUM MOTIF

ROUND 1: *(Right Side)* Starting with first color, ch 4 join to first ch to form ring; ch 3, [dc in ring] 15 times; join to first dc *(3rd ch of beg ch-3).* (16 dc) Fasten off.

ROUND 2: Join next color with sl st to any dc, ch 3, dc in same st as joining, [2 dc in next dc] around; join to first dc *(3rd ch of beg ch-3).* (32 dc) Fasten off.

Note: When working in the back loops, I suggest working through the back loop together with the loop below the back loop (third loop). This makes the stitch more stable and doesn't leave any holes.

ROUND 3: Using next color, join with sc to **back loop** of any dc, working in **back loops** only, [sc in next dc] around; join to first sc. (32 sc) Fasten off.

SMALL MOTIF

ROUND 1: Repeat Rnd 1 of Large Motif. Fasten off.

ASSEMBLY OF GARLAND – Use photo as guide

Note: *The number of chains used to start and end the garland, as well as the number of chains between joining the Motifs, is entirely up to you.*

Using Main Color, ch 50, *sc in center hdc of any 3-hdc group on Large Motif, ch 20, sc in any dc on Small Motif, ch 20, sc in any sc on Medium Motif, ch 20, sc in any dc on Small Motif**, ch 20; rep from * until all Motifs are joined, ch 50. Fasten off.

Large Motif

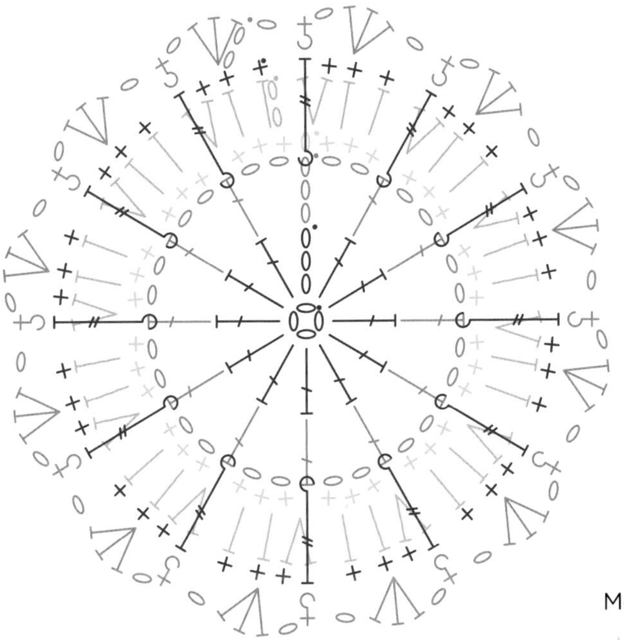

Small Motif

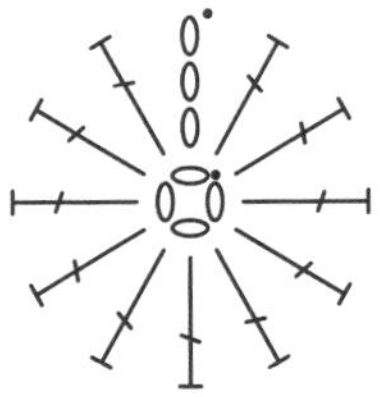

Medium Motif

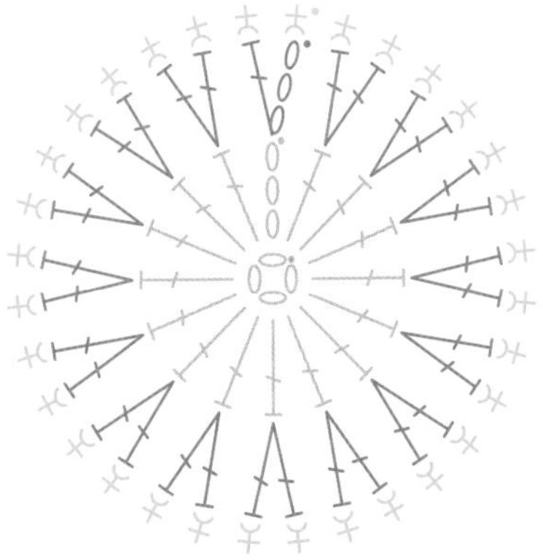

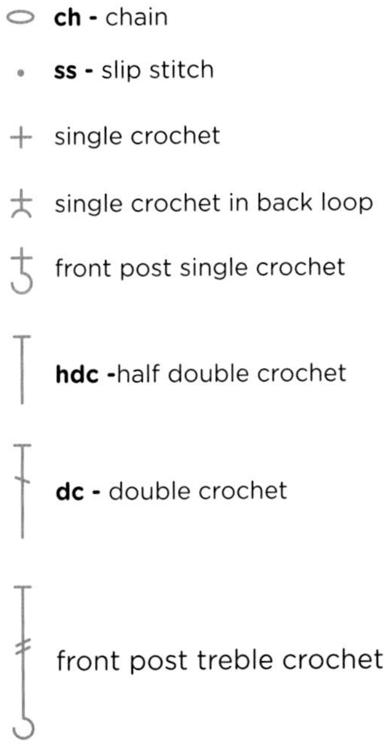
ch - chain
ss - slip stitch
single crochet
single crochet in back loop
front post single crochet
hdc -half double crochet
dc - double crochet
front post treble crochet

PINEAPPLES AND LACE CUSHION

The majority of my crochet designs are not of the 'lacey' type. There are many beautiful doilies out there made from the finest cotton, giving them the appearance of lace. So, I wanted to try something a little different and make a doily-type cushion. I do believe that using an insert with (or covering the insert with) a contrasting colored fabric, would make the cushion pop quite nicely. Both sides of the cushion cover are the same, and they work up a lot quicker than what you would think. The two sides are woven together using a length of chain stitches.

Finished Size

To fit 16" (40 cm) round cushion

FINISHED SIZE

To fit 16" (40 cm) round cushion

MATERIALS

DMC Natura Just Cotton

Main Color – Malva (#31) 2 balls

Hook: Size E-4 (3.50 mm)

Scissors & Yarn Needle

16" (40 cm) Round Pillow Form

PATTERN NOTES

1 A Magic Ring *(see Techniques)* can be used instead of the chain ring in Round 1.

2 All joins are slip stitches, unless otherwise indicated.3.

3 All new colors are joined with right side facing, unless otherwise indicated.

4 Weave in all ends as you go.

5 Standing stitches *(see Techniques)* can be used to start a round with a new color.

6 An invisible join *(see Techniques)* can be used at the end of a round to finish a color.

SPECIAL STITCHES

Back Post Double Crochet (BPdc): Yarn over hook, insert hook from back to front to back around post of indicated stitch, yarn over and draw up loop, [yarn over and pull through 2 loops] twice (double crochet made).

Popcorn (pc): Work 5 dc in same stitch or space indicated, drop lp from hook, insert hook from front to back in first dc made, pull dropped lp through, ch 1 (to lock).

V-Stitch (v-st): Work (dc, ch 1, dc) in same stitch or space indicated.

CUSHION COVER

SIDES – Make 2

ROUND 1: *(Right Side)* Starting with Main Color, ch 8; join to first ch to form ring; ch 3 (counts as first dc, now and throughout), 23 dc in ring; join to first dc *(3rd ch of beg ch-3)*. (24 dc) Fasten off.

ROUND 2: Ch 1, sc in next dc, [ch 4, sl st in 2nd ch from hook *(picot made)*, ch 3, skip next 2 dc, sc in next dc] 7 times, ch 3; join with dc in first sc *(to form last loop and position yarn)*, ch 1 *(as picot)*. (8 sc, 8 loops with picots)

ROUND 3: Ch 6 *(counts as first dc & ch-3, now and throughout)*, 2 dc in last ch-1 *(as picot)* on Rnd 2, ch 2, [(2 dc, ch 3, 2 dc) in next picot, ch 2] around, ending with dc in same first picot; join to first dc *(3rd ch of beg ch-6)*. (32 dc, 8 ch-3 sps & 16 ch-2 sps)

ROUND 4: Sl st in next ch-3 sp, ch 7 *(counts as first dc & ch-4)*, (pc, ch 3, dc) in same sp, ch 2, [(dc, ch 4, pc, ch 3, dc) in next ch-3 sp, ch 2] around; join to first dc *(3rd ch of beg ch-7)*. (16 dc, 8 popcorns, 8 ch-4 lps, 8 ch-3 lps & 8 ch-2 sps)

ROUND 5: Ch 1 *(loosely)*, [5 dc in next ch-4 lp, ch 1, 5 dc in next ch-3 lp, ch 2] around; join to first dc. (80 dc, 8 ch-1 sps & 8 ch-2 sps)

ROUND 6: Sl st in each of next 4 dc, sl st in next ch-1 sp, ch 6, dc in same sp, *ch 4, skip next 5 dc, **v-st** *(see Special Stitches)* in next ch-2 sp, ch 4, skip next 5 dc**, (dc, ch 3, dc) in next ch-1 sp; rep from * around, ending at ** on final repeat; join to first dc (3rd ch of beg ch-6). (8 v-sts, 16 dc, 8 ch-3 sps & 16 ch-4 sps)

ROUND 7: Sl st in next ch-3 sp, ch 4 *(counts as first tr, now and throughout)*, 7 tr in same sp, *ch 3, v-st in next v-st, ch 3**, 8 tr in next ch-3 sp; rep from * around, ending at ** on final repeat; join to first tr *(4th ch of beg ch-4)*. (64 tr, 8 v-sts & 16 ch-3 sps)

ROUND 8: Ch 5 *(counts as first tr & ch-1)*, tr in next tr, [ch 1, tr in next tr] 6 times, *ch 2, v-st in next v-st, ch 2**, tr in next tr, [ch 1, tr in next tr] 7 times; rep from * around, ending at ** on final repeat; join to first tr *(4th ch of beg ch-5)*. (64 tr, 8 v-sts, 16 ch-2 sps & 56 ch-1 sps)

ROUND 9: Ch 1, *sc in next ch-1 sp, [ch 3, sc in next ch-1 sp] 6 times, ch 3, v-st in next v-st, ch 3; rep from * around; join to first sc. (56 sc, 48 ch-3 lps, 8 v-sts & 16 ch-3 sps)

ROUND 10: Ch 1, *sc in next ch-1 sp, [ch 3, sc in next ch-1 sp] 5 times, ch 3, (v-st, ch 1, dc) in next v-st, ch 3; rep from * around; join to first sc. (48 sc, 40 ch-3 lps, 8 v-sts & 16 ch-3 sps)

ROUND 11: Ch 1, *sc in next ch-1 sp, [ch 3, sc in next ch-1 sp] 4 times, ch 2, (2 dc, ch 1, 2 dc) in each of next 2 ch-1 sps, ch 2; rep from * around; join to first sc. (40 sc, 32 ch-3 lps, 64 dc, 16 ch-1 sps & 16 ch-2 sps)

ROUND 12: Ch 1, *sc in next ch-1 sp, [ch 3, sc in next ch-1 sp] 3 times, ch 3, (dc, ch 1, pc, dc) in next ch-1 sp, ch 2, (dc, ch 1, pc, dc) in next ch-1 sp, ch 3; rep from * around; join to first sc. (32 sc, 24 ch-3 lps, 32 dc, 16 popcorns, 8 ch-2 sps, 32 ch-1 sps & 16 ch-3 sps)

ROUND 13: Ch 1, *sc in next ch-1 sp, [ch 3, sc in next ch-1 sp] twice, ch 3, [2 dc in next ch-1 sp, ch 1] twice, pc in next ch-2 sp, [ch 1, 2 dc in next ch-1 sp] twice, ch 3; rep from * around; join to first sc. (24 sc, 16 ch-3 lps, 64 dc, 8 popcorns, 32 ch-1 sps & 16 ch-3 sps)

ROUND 14: Ch 1, *sc in next ch-1 sp, ch 3, sc in next ch-1 sp, ch 3, dc in each of next 2 dc, ch 2, skip ch-sp, dc in each of next 2 dc, ch 6, skip pc, dc in each of next 2 dc, ch 2, skip ch-sp, dc in each of next 2 dc, ch 3; rep from * around; join to first sc. (16 sc, 8 ch-3 lps, 64 dc, 8 ch-6 lps, 16 ch-2 sps & 16 ch-3 sps)

ROUND 15: Sl st in next ch-3 sp, ch 6 *(counts as first tr & ch-2)*, *skip ch-sp, dc in each of next 2 dc, 2 hdc in next ch-2 sp, hdc in each of next 2 dc, 6 sc in next ch-6 lp, hdc in each of next 2 dc, 2 hdc in next ch-2 sp, dc in each of

next 2 dc, ch 2**, (tr, ch 3, tr) in next ch-3 lp; rep from * around, ending at ** on final repeat, tr in same first ch 3 lp; join with dc to first tr *(4th ch of beg ch-6)* to form last ch-3 lp. (16 tr, 8 ch-3 lps, 32 dc, 64 hdc, 48 sc & 16 ch-2 sps)

ROUND 16: Ch 1, sc in lp under hook, *ch 5, skip ch-sp, sc in next dc, ch 6, skip next 4 sts, sc in next hdc, ch 8, skip next 6 sc, sc in next hdc, ch 6, skip next 4 sts, sc in next dc**, ch 5, sc in next ch-3 lp; rep from * around, ending at ** on final repeat; ch 2, join with dc to first sc *(to form last ch-5 lp)*. (40 sc, 16 ch-5 lps, 16 ch-6 lps & 8 ch-8 lps)

ROUND 17: Ch 1, sc in lp under hook, *ch 6, sc in next ch-lp] around, ending with ch 3; join with dc to first sc *(to form last ch-6 lp)*. (40 sc & 40 ch-6 lps)

ROUND 18: Ch 1, sc in lp under hook, *ch 7, sc in next ch-lp] around, ending with ch 3; join with tr to first sc *(to form last ch-7 lp)*. (40 sc & 40 ch-7 lps)

ROUND 19: Ch 1, sc in lp under hook, *ch 8, sc in next ch-lp] around, ending with ch 4; join with tr to first sc *(to form last ch-7 lp)*. (40 sc & 40 ch-8 lps) Fasten off and weave in all ends.

TIE
With Main Color, ch 500. Fasten off and weave in all ends.

ASSEMBLY – Use photo as guide

Place Pillow Form between both Cover Sides, with right sides facing (wrong sides against pillow form), matching stitches, weave Tie through adjoining ch-8 lps around Cover. Tie ends of Tie together in a bow (or weave in ends).

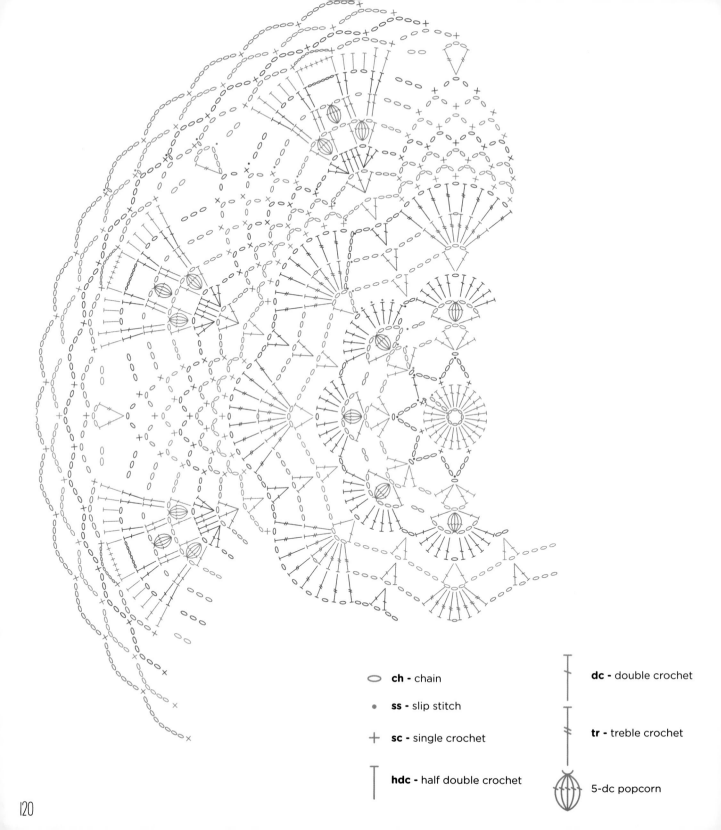

ch - chain

ss - slip stitch

sc - single crochet

hdc - half double crochet

dc - double crochet

tr - treble crochet

5-dc popcorn

CROCHET BASICS AND TECHNIQUES

CROCHET BASICS

SLIP KNOT

Almost every crochet project starts with a slip knot on the hook. This is not mentioned in any pattern – it is assumed.

To make a slip knot, form a loop with your yarn (the tail end hanging behind your loop); insert the hook through the loop, and pick up the ball end of the yarn. Draw yarn through loop. Keeping loop on hook, gently tug the tail end to tighten the knot. Tugging the ball end tightens the loop.

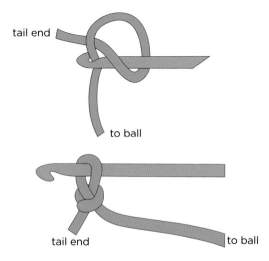

YARN OVER (yo)

This is a common practice, especially with the taller stitches.

With a loop on your hook, wrap the yarn (attached to the ball) from back to front around the shaft of your hook.

CHAIN STITCH (ch)

The chain stitch is the foundation of most crochet projects.

The foundation chain is a series of chain stitches in which you work the first row of stitches.

To make a chain stitch, you start with a slip knot (or loop) on the hook. Yarn over and pull the yarn through the loop on your hook (first chain stitch made). For more chain stitches, repeat: Yarn over, pull through loop on hook.

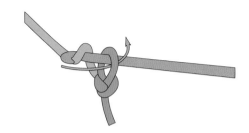

Hint: Don't pull the stitches too tight, otherwise they will be difficult to work in.

When counting chain stitches, do not count the slip knot, nor the loop on the hook. Only count the number of 'v's.

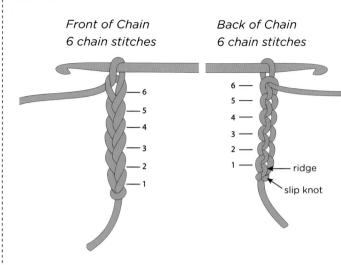

Front of Chain
6 chain stitches

Back of Chain
6 chain stitches

SLIP STITCH (sl st)

Starting with a loop on your hook, insert hook in stitch or space specified and pull up a loop, pulling it through the loop on your hook as well.

The slip stitch is commonly used to attach new yarn and to join rounds.

Attaching a New Color or New Ball of Yarn (or Joining with a Slip Stitch (join with sl st)).

Make a slip knot with the new color (or yarn) and place loop on hook. Insert hook from front to back in the (usually) first stitch (unless specified otherwise). Yarn over and pull loop through stitch and loop on hook (slip stitch made).

SINGLE CROCHET (sc)

Starting with a loop on your hook, insert hook in stitch or space specified and draw up a loop (two loops on hook). Yarn over and pull yarn through both the loops on your hook (first sc made).

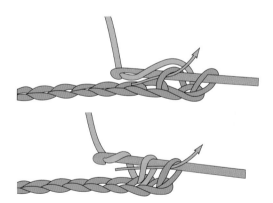

The height of a single crochet stitch is one chain high.

When working single crochet stitches into a foundation chain, begin the first single crochet in the second chain from the hook. The skipped chain stitch provides the height of the stitch.

At the beginning of a single crochet row or round, start by making one chain stitch (to get the height) and work the first single crochet stitch into first stitch (***Note:*** The one chain stitch is never counted as a single crochet stitch).

HALF-DOUBLE CROCHET (hdc)

Starting with a loop on your hook, yarn over hook before inserting hook in stitch or space specified and draw up a loop (three loops on hook). Yarn over and pull yarn through all three loops (first hdc made).

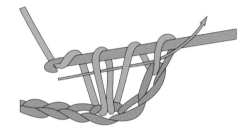

The height of a half-double crochet stitch is two chains high.

When working half-double crochet stitches into a foundation chain, begin the first stitch in the third chain from the hook. The two skipped chains provide the height. When starting a row or round with a half-double crochet stitch, make two chain stitches and work in the first stitch (Note: The two chain stitches are never counted as a half-double stitch).

DOUBLE CROCHET (dc)

Starting with a loop on your hook, yarn over hook before inserting hook in stitch or space specified and draw up a loop (three loops on hook). Yarn over and pull yarn through two loops (two loops remain on hook). Yarn over and pull yarn through remaining two loops on hook (first dc made).
The height of a double crochet stitch is three chains high.

When working double crochet stitches into a foundation chain, begin the first stitch in the fourth chain from the hook.

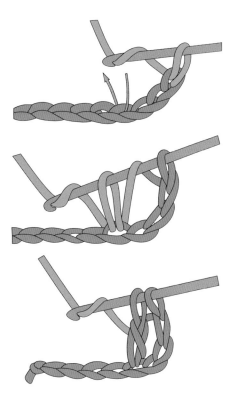

The three skipped chains count as the first double crochet stitch. When starting a row or round with a double crochet stitch, make three chain stitches (which count as the first

double crochet), skip the first stitch (under the chains) and work a double crochet in the next (second) stitch. On the following row or round, when you work in the 'made' stitch, you will be working in the top chain (3rd chain stitch of the three chains).

TREBLE (OR TRIPLE) CROCHET (tr)

Starting with a loop on your hook, yarn over hook twice before inserting hook in stitch or space specified and draw up a loop (four loops on hook). Yarn over and pull yarn through two loops (three loops remain on hook). Again, make a yarn over and pull yarn through two loops (two loops remain on hook). Once more, yarn over and pull through remaining two loops (first tr made).

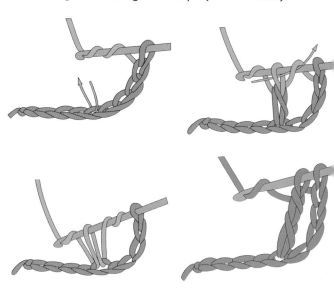

The height of a treble crochet stitch is four chains high. When working treble crochet stitches into a foundation chain, begin the first stitch in the fifth chain from the hook. The four skipped chains count as the first treble crochet stitch. When starting a row or round with a treble crochet stitch, make four chain stitches (which count as the first treble crochet), skip the first stitch (under the chains) and work a treble crochet in the next (second) stitch. On the following row or round, when you work in the 'made' stitch, you will be working in the top chain (4th chain stitch of the four chains).

DOUBLE TREBLE (OR DOUBLE TRIPLE) CROCHET (dtr)

Starting with a loop on your hook, yarn over hook three times before inserting hook in stitch or space specified and draw up a loop (five loops on hook). *Yarn over and pull yarn through two loops; rep from * three times more (until only the loop on your hook remains (first dtr made).

The height of a double treble crochet stitch is five chains high.

HEIGHT OF CHAIN STITCHES

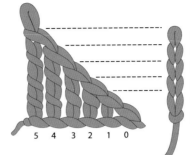

5 Double Treble Crochet
4 Treble Crochet
3 Double Crochet
2 Half-Double Crochet
1 Single Crochet
0 Slip Stitch

CROCHET TECHNIQUES

MAGIC RING
Instead of starting with a ring consisting of a number of chain stitches, one can use a Magic Ring.

You start as if you were making a slip knot: Form a loop with your yarn (the tail end hanging behind your loop); insert the hook through the loop, and pick up the ball end of the yarn. Draw yarn through loop. Here is where things change… Do not tighten up the knot or loop. Make a chain stitch (to 'lock' the ring), then continue with the 'height' chain stitches. Work the required stitches into the ring (over the tail strand). When all the stitches are done, gently tug the tail end to close the ring, before joining the round (if specified). Remember, make sure this tail is firmly secured when weaving in the end.

STANDING STITCHES
Standing stitches replace the normal "join a new color (or yarn) with a slip stitch to the stitch or space specified and then chain up to the stitch height". They are made by working the stitch from the top-down.

Single Crochet Stitch Standing Stitch (join with sc)
With slip knot on hook, insert hook into stitch or space indicated and pull up a loop (two loops on hook). Yarn over and pull through both loops on hook (first single crochet made).

Half-Double Crochet Standing Stitch
With slip knot on hook, yarn over, (holding the two loops with thumb) insert hook into stitch or space indicated and pull up a loop (three loops on hook). Yarn over and pull through all three loops (standing half-double crochet made).

Double Crochet Standing Stitch
With slip knot on hook, yarn over, (holding the two loops with thumb) insert hook into stitch or space indicated and pull up a loop (three loops on hook). Yarn over and pull through two loop (two loops on hook). Yarn over and pull through remaining two loops (standing double crochet made).

CHANGING COLORS / ATTACHING NEW YARN

Changing to a new ball of yarn or a new color, ideally should happen when starting a new row or round.
Instead of fastening off one color and then joining a new color with a slip stitch or Standing Stitch, one can use the following technique:

In the stitch before the change, work up to last step of the stitch (In most cases the last step of a stitch is the final "yarn over, pull through remaining stitches on hook"). This is where the change happens. Here you will use the new color in the "yarn over" and pull it through the remaining stitches.

This technique is not only used for color changing. It can also be used to introduce a new ball of yarn (of the same color) while working on a project.

BACK RIDGE OF FOUNDATION CHAIN

Most projects start with a foundation chain – a string of chain stitches. One can identify the front of the chain stitches by seeing 'v's. When you turn the foundation chain over, at the back are a string of 'bumps'. This is referred to as the back ridge (or back bar) of the chain.

When working in the back ridge of the chain stitches, one inserts the hook from front to back through the 'bar' (the 'v' is underneath the hook) and pulls the yarn through the 'bar'.

Working your first row in the back ridge of the foundation chain, gives a neat finish to your project. If you are seaming pieces together, it also creates a flatter seam.

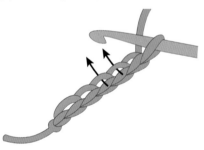

FRONT AND BACK LOOPS

Each stitch has what we call 'v's on the top. Unless otherwise specified, all stitches are worked by inserting the hook under both the loops – under the 'v'.
Sometimes a pattern calls for stitches worked in either the front or back loops. These are the two loops that make up the 'v'. The front loops are the loops closest to you and the back loops are the loops furthest from you. Working in the front or back loops only, creates a decorative ridge (of the unworked loops).

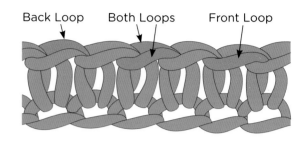

THIRD LOOPS

Besides the Back and Front Loops of any basic stitch, there is also a 'third loop'. This loop looks like a horizontal bar and is found at the back of the stitch. When the 'v's of the stitches are facing you, it is found behind the back loop. When the 'v's are facing away from you, it is the loop below the front loop. Working stitches into the third loop, creates a decorative line of 'v's.

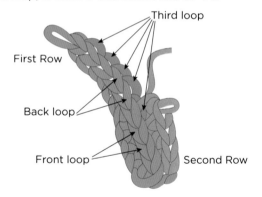

CRAB STITCH

This stitch is also known as Reverse Single Crochet (rev-sc) and creates a neat edging to a project. It is similar to the regular single crochet stitch but is worked in the opposite direction – left to right (for right-handers) and right to left (for left-handers).

With a loop on the hook, * insert hook in next st to the right (or left for left-handers) and pull up loop, yarn over and pull through both loops on hook. Repeat from * across (or around).

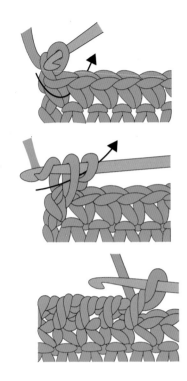

SURFACE STITCHES

These decorative stiches look like embroidered chain stitches.

Make a slip knot. Insert hook as specified in pattern from front (right side) to back (wrong side) of fabric. Place slip knot on hook (at back). Keeping the yarn to the back, pull the loop of the slip knot through to the front (keeping the knot at the back). *Insert hook in next spot specified (from front to back), pull up yarn through fabric and through loop on hook (slip stitch). Repeat from * as per pattern.

JOINING SEAMS

There are many ways ways to join your crochet pieces together. Once all your crocheted motifs or pieces are finished, you can choose to:

1) Sew them together, using needle and yarn, matching stitches and rows where possible. There are various sewing stitches you can use, the most common one being the whip-stitch.

2) Crochet the seams together, using either a slip stitch or a row of single crochet stitches. These can be worked from the wrong side or can be used decoratively on the right side of the fabric. Another crocheted seam is the flat 'Zipper Join' (see below).

3) A third method, "join-as-you-go", is what it says. While you're crocheting on one piece, you're joining it to an already finished piece. Generally, the join is a slip stitch worked into a chain space on the finished piece. When there are no chain spaces available, another technique is PLT – "pull loop through" (see below).

Zipper Join

This join is worked on the right side of the fabric and the chain created by the slip stitches lies flat in the 'ditch' between the front loops of both pieces.
With both pieces of fabric lying side by side – right sides facing, *insert hook from front to back through back loop on the first and then repeat in the corresponding stitch on the other piece, yarn over and pull yarn through both stitches and the loop on hook (slip stitch made). Repeat from * across.
Whenever you come to an intersection of another seam, make a chain stitch and skip the seam. Continue with the zipper join on the other side of the seam.

When you need to decrease stitches while working the zipper join, on the side that needs decreasing, you insert hook from front to back through each of the next two stitches. The yarn is then pulled through three stitches (one single stitch on one side and two stitches on the decrease side) together with the loop on hook.

PLT Pull Loop Through

Working with both pieces right sides facing, on the current piece, make the loop on hook slightly larger and remove the hook. Insert hook from front to back through the corresponding stitch on the finished piece and pick up the loop and pull it through the stitch. Then continue working in the current piece until you need to join again.

BLOCKING

To give your crochet creations a beautiful and professional look, it is advisable to block them all when finished. You can also block motifs before joining them together.

Wet-blocking is done by pinning out your piece to size and shape (using non-rust pins) on a clean, flat and soft surface. You can use towels, foam board, or rubber mat tiles.

Depending on the yarn you used, you can gently wash your crochet pieces first and then pin them out, or you can pin out the dry pieces, and lightly spritz them with water, or (if they are NOT acrylic) hover a steam iron over them. Never let the iron touch the crochet pieces. Leave the pinned pieces to dry completely.

THANK YOU

This book has taken me on an incredible journey, where I have met amazing people, formed life-long friendships and learned so much more than I ever thought possible. And I could not have done this all on my own! I had the help and assistance of so many incredible people.

First and foremost, I want to thank Tuva Publishing for giving me this unbelievable opportunity to write my own book. It has been such a wonderful experience working with you throughout this journey. From receiving the very first email, which I re- and re-read over and over in amazement, to all the other emails exchanged back and forth. Thank you, Kader, for making this dream of mine a reality. Your support and guidance throughout has been something I will always remember and cherish. I would also like to share my sincere gratitude and thanks to Wendi for all her hard work. I am lucky to have been able to share this process with you. Thank you for making this journey more memorable.

My dream of becoming an author became even more real the moment a parcel of luscious yarn arrived on my doorstep. So, a very big 'thank-you' to DMC for providing all the wonderful, colorful yarn to inspire me.

I'm forever grateful to all the wonderful Testers that shared this journey with me. Thanks to them, all the work they did, and all the support they gave me, this book has managed to come to fruition. In no particular order and with heartfelt gratitude, I would love to thank: Angela, Kirsten, Ann-Mari, Courtney, Juliette, Ally, Sue Ellen, Natalie, Amy, Kate, Heather, Glenyse, Deb, Jenna, Sam, Narelle, Jess,

Jenaya, Megan, Angela, Margaret, Anna, and Ritha. And a special 'thank-you' to Zoe for helping me find the right words for the book's blurb as well as for the title of my book. I love you all!

Thank-you Aunty Fiona and Barbara, for opening your doors and letting me use your beautiful homes as backdrops to my designs.

Another big 'thank-you' to Terrii, who was always there no matter the time of day or night. Your words of wisdom and advice will continue to ring true. And I will be forever grateful. I am so glad to call you my friend.

To my younger sister, Lara, thank you for making our photo session such fun and for being a wonderful model. I am truly grateful for all your help.

Last, but not least, the most special thanks goes to my family and close friends. I have been in my crochet bubble for a long time and I thank you all for your patience and support. Your encouragement and faith in my abilities made this journey one I will never forget. I am so lucky to have you as my family. I want to immensely thank you, Richard (my other half), for your help, words of wisdom, and always keeping the boys occupied, so that I could finish 'that last round'. You are my rock and without your support I would not have ventured down this path. Your acceptance of my crocheting will never be forgotten.

Love,
Emily xo